LEGACY

Charleston, SC
www.PalmettoPublishing.com

Legacy

First Edition

Hardcover: 979-8-8229-0308-1
Paperback: 979-8-8229-0309-8

Legacy

ROBERT BLICK

The angel said to me, "These words are trustworthy and true. The Lord, the God who inspires the prophets, sent his angel to show his servants the things that must soon take place."

—Revelations 22:6

Table of Contents

CHAPTER 1:

The Shooting

The roll call for the First District of the Saint Louis Metropolitan Police Department for the afternoon watch was very similar to other recent roll calls. Three more officers had called in sick due to the most recent COVID-variant virus. In fact, the entire department was struggling to fill cars on all three watches every day. Sergeant David Boyer knew the potential challenges ahead, so he decided he would jump in with one of his officers to help handle assignments for tonight's tour of duty.

Sergeant David Boyer, forty years old, had been on the force for almost nineteen years and would often think, Is there life after police work? Boyer enjoyed being a city cop; in fact, he loved it! A lot of days were stressful, and his day-to-day interactions with people often intersected with crazy, disturbing, or illegal behavior. Then there were those days when he actually did solid, positive police work and "protected and served" the citizens of Saint Louis. He knew he was in the right job for now. Just last week, Sergeant Boyer and two of his younger patrolmen worked in conjunction with Robbery Division to locate and arrest a former convict who was carjacking SUVs in the Marketplace parking lot. Boyer knew he was no hero, but that day felt very satisfying as those folks in that neighborhood were just a little bit safer due to his and his rookies' hard work.

Veteran officer Charlie Hennessey suddenly stood at Sergeant Boyer's doorway to his office. "Hey, Sarge, what was that attorney's name that was working the Brookfield case last summer?"

"Hays…Andrew Hays," Sergeant Boyer replied.

"Oh yeah, I keep forgetting," Hennessey murmured.

"Hays, like Rutherford B. Hayes," the sergeant clarified.

"Who?"

"The nineteenth president of the United States, right after Grant, just before Garfield," Boyer said with a sardonic smile.

"Oh, OK." Hennessey looked confused.

"Or like Willie Mays Hayes, the speedster from Charlie Sheen and Tom Berenger's *Major League*," Boyer said sarcastically.

"Oh yeah, I remember him. Good movie!" Charlie replied. "He was a good outfielder."

"Don't you have some reports to work on, Hennessey?"

"Right, on it, Sarge," Hennessey said, leaving the area quickly.

Sergeant Boyer had an extraordinary memory. He could remember volumes of history, including the dates, the places, and the historical figures. He knew the Bible, sports, geography, and current events inside out. Boyer could remember the first and last names of most people he met on the streets and in the neighborhoods. If you needed someone for trivia night, David Boyer would be your first choice!

Working the afternoon shift did have its challenges as it prevented him from spending quality time with his wife, Clarissa, and his three teenage daughters: Staci, nineteen; Jennifer, eighteen; and Sadie, sixteen. The girls all played club volleyball, and his two younger daughters, Jennifer and Sadie, swam for the Midwest Aquatic Club. Clarissa—or Rissa, as he called her—was a star mom, who drove the girls to all the matches and meets. She would sit hours on the uncomfortable benches and chairs in the local gyms and swimming centers. In addition, Rissa worked thirty-five hours a week as a paralegal with a law firm downtown, a job she loved. How she found time for everything was truly amazing.

The temperature had finally gotten cooler as mid-October approached. The Saint Louis Cardinals season was over as they lost in the first round of the National League playoff to the San Diego Padres. Sergeant Boyer was actually glad the long season was over; Busch Stadium was taxing his officers that worked all that secondary. Sergeant Boyer's phone buzzed. Officer William Howard, two years on the force, texted he was not feeling well and would not be in tonight. That was the fourth patrolman out tonight, which would make for some interesting car assignments at roll call.

Boyer went down the hall to check in with Lieutenant Gerald Adams.

"Afternoon, LT," Sergeant Boyer said, poking his head in Adams's cramped and cluttered office. "Four guys out tonight—thinking I would ride with Sullivan. Too much going on out there to be shorthanded."

"OK, Sergeant, just make sure that the department accident report is done by tomorrow. I need to review it as soon as possible," Adams muttered, barely looking up from his desk.

Sergeant Boyer did not mind riding tonight, as it had been a while since he had run the streets, and he was looking forward to the evening. Doing paperwork and officer evals was OK but had gotten a little old of late. Besides, he was riding with Officer Mike Sullivan, a friend—or at least someone who used to be a friend when they rode together before Boyer became sergeant. The recent years of being his boss had probably separated their friendship. There was no fallout or anything like that—it's a natural distancing that occurs when you no longer ride with a guy or assign him protection duty for the state senator on a holiday weekend. Guy friendship can be tough stuff—it's just the way it is.

The afternoon roll call was always in the dank basement conference room of the old brick building off Sublette Avenue. The squeaky duct-taped chairs seemed ancient and were always uncomfortable to sit in for more than a few minutes. The officers typically sat there quietly, listening to the watch commander's communication of what might be a threat or point of interest that evening. After the communication, Sergeant Boyer's roll call was uneventful, other than moving around some officers due to the sick call-ins and advising all to be aware of the recent spikes in burglaries in the area. Boyer asked if there were any questions. No one spoke, and the officers were dismissed. Mike Sullivan approached his sergeant.

"So, do I need to show you how to use the new feature on the body cam tonight, Sarge?" snarked Officer Sullivan.

"I am good," Boyer responded. "But you can buy me tacos at Roberto's on Fyler tonight."

"Will do. See you at the car in five, OK?" said Sullivan.

Sergeant Boyer nodded, glancing at some departmental news on his cell phone. Nothing of major interest. Hopefully, it would be a slow and peaceful night. As he walked toward the police garage, his mind wandered back to the first day at the old police academy building off Clark Street. Most of the cadets like himself had seemed so young, so nervous. Boyer got along with his peers well, and they in turn seemed to like the young athletic-looking cadet. He excelled in law, ethics, report writing, and traffic in the classroom. It was the daily runs, however, where Boyer was getting noticed by his peers and instructors. He remembered running his first timed training mile at 5:10 on that muggy upstairs track. He thought that he knew everything and the next twelve weeks would be a breeze.

His thoughts shifted to before the academy, to how the first year at University of Kansas did not work out. Sure, the partial academic scholarship was great and helped his parents out on the financial burden. What was he thinking, however, that he could simply walk on the Jayhawk freshman football team and start that first season?

After one year in Lawrence, he was struggling, with football, with his classes, with everything. He had to get out; he missed home. What a blessing it was to accidentally run into Ryan Thomas, his old buddy from high school, at the Cardinals game. Ryan had recently joined the city police department and could not stop talking about how he loved the job, loved the rush. David Boyer knew right then and there he was going to have a new purpose, a new start in life: he would join the police department.

A few months out of the police academy, he met Rissa. He was invited to go to a new church by one of his fellow officers who had graduated with him, and after the service, he was introduced to this pretty blonde. She was very bubbly and talked about her love for sports, her passion for the law, and her six-month stay in the UK for an international studies program at Northwestern. David did not hear much of her stories that day as he was mesmerized by her stunning looks. They got married six months later and rented a small one-bedroom apartment in south Saint Louis. They started attending a local nondenominational church ten minutes from where they lived. Both David and Clarissa accepted Jesus soon after, and South City Christian Church was the right fit for them.

"Sarge, you ready? Don't be daydreaming when riding with me tonight," laughed Mike Sullivan. "Head on a swivel, isn't that what you always told me?"

The first part of the evening was relaxing, and they both enjoyed the light, cool breeze indicating fall had arrived. It was good to catch up with Mike and what was new with his family. Mike had two boys, both very good junior high school football players in the Webster school district. His wife, Christine, was a registered nurse and had been working a ton of hours lately.

"Christine is always exhausted when she comes home," Mike said. "I get it, I really do, but even getting her to do stuff, to go out to dinner, is a chore of late."

"Yeah, RNs and doctors probably have it tougher than us these days. You just have to be patient, Mike; this virus thing can't last forever," Sergeant Boyer said, trying to be reassuring.

Boyer glanced at the silver medal of Saint Michael the Archangel, patron saint of police officers, hanging from the rearview mirror.

"You know, you guys are welcome to come to church this Sunday with us. Rissa would love to see Christine, and the message is on patience and understanding for husbands of registered nurses!"

"Very funny, Sarge," Mike snickered. "Christine works late Saturday and not sure she wants to get up early for the two-hour service."

"It's only an hour, and Catholics can leave early if they so desire," Boyer laughed.

Marie Lazzeri, District 1 Dispatcher, was indiscreetly flipping through her Facebook page on her Apple iPhone 13, sipping on her second Coke Zero of her shift, when she got pinged in the call queue. A ticket came through by a 911 operator communicating there was an armed burglary in progress. Marie quickly processed the information and went to work.

"Twenty-one twenty-four, twenty-one eleven," Marie said, alerting both Officer Sullivan and Sergeant Boyer.

"Twenty-one twenty-four," Officer Sullivan responded.

"Respond to a burglary in progress, 2712 Bates Street, Fiore's Jewelers. Two subjects—one white, one black—inside the store, maybe armed. Twenty-one twenty-four, you will have the assignment. All District 1 cars be advised to respond," Marie broadcasted

"Twenty-one twenty-four, twenty-one eleven responding, two minutes out." said Sergeant Boyer. Neither man said anything as Officer Sullivan raced the new Chevy Tahoe through the south side city toward the jewelry store.

"Once we arrive, I will go in first," Sergeant Boyer said firmly.

"Got it. Hit that body cam as soon as you exit, Sarge," Sullivan reminded his old partner.

The patrol SUV, lights flashing, skidded to a stop twenty feet from the front entrance of Fiore's. Sergeant Boyer quickly exited the SUV with Sullivan a few seconds behind him. Boyer pushed open the glass door. "Police!" shouted the sergeant. The jewelry store's large, dimly lit interior was empty, glass scattered across the floor. Standing in a corner behind a broken watch case was Vincent Fiore, the elderly owner.

He was obviously shaken but managed to weakly say, "Thank God, police. The thugs went out the back door, into the alley."

"Are you hurt?" asked Sergeant Boyer.

"No, but—but my store—they took…" Tears started streaming down the man's cheek.

"Stay right here, more officers are coming." Boyer said calmly to the older jeweler.

Figuring Mr. Fiore would be OK until backup arrived, both Boyer and Sullivan hurried through the back door of the old shop and into the narrow alley. About one hundred feet from the back entrance, they saw two young men with backpacks running north in the alley. Sergeant Boyer and Officer Sullivan started running after the burglars. Boyer slowed momentarily, lowered his chin, and spoke into his mic on his right shoulder.

"Twenty-one twenty-four, twenty-one eleven on scene. No one appears hurt inside Fiore's. Two suspects—one white, one black—both wearing hoodies and backpacks left the scene. Now in the alley, behind the store, headed north toward South Grand Boulevard, pursuing on foot."

Officer Sullivan, now ahead of his sergeant still running hard, saw the suspects were getting close to South Grand, giving them several options in their escape as this was a busy street. At South Grand, the young men split up. Black Hoodie went right, and Sullivan stopped for a second, looked behind, and saw Sergeant Boyer twenty yards behind but catching up quickly.

"I'm going right!" Sullivan shouted and turned the corner, continuing the chase. Sergeant Boyer arrived at South Grand seconds later and could see the second suspect ahead, with a slim build and gray hoodie, looking over his shoulder often as he ran.

"Police, stop!" shouted Sergeant Boyer. He felt the nine-millimeter Beretta 92F in his left hand—it felt light—as he ran. No more five-minute academy runs, but David felt fast that night. He would catch this guy. Gray Hoodie darted left into another narrow alley.

"Stupid alleys," Sergeant Boyer said under his breath as he neared his turn.

"Breathe," he said out loud, running hard as he turned the corner.

Just to his right about ten yards ahead, Boyer saw Gray Hoodie partially hidden behind a dirty green dumpster.

"Police! Let me see your hands!" Sergeant Boyer screamed out, bringing up his Beretta.

Just then he heard loud cracks, saw a flash, and felt an immediate blow to his upper chest. A second later, a warm sensation emitted from his throat. Sergeant Boyer crashed to the pavement. Things got really confusing for the sergeant in a hurry—he could not breathe well, and he knew he was bleeding badly from his neck. Boyer was going in and out of consciousness. For a few seconds, he could hear a few distinct sounds: a dog barking, sirens blaring, a woman shouting. Then all would go quiet as if he had his Bose headphones on, drowning out every sound.

As Sergeant Boyer lay in the alley, he faintly heard a voice saying, "Officer shot, officer down." He thought he saw Mike bending over him, felt his hands on his neck, talking fast, talking loudly—something about "Stay with me, Sarge."

Officer Mike Sullivan knew Sergeant Boyer was losing a lot of blood. He kept his hands on the wound on his sergeant's throat. The body armor over his chest had protected Boyer from the first shot; the neck wound, however, appeared very serious. His neck and shoulders were soaked with blood. Sullivan wondered how long he could stop some of the bleeding before the paramedics arrived.

"Sarge, I got you, help is coming," Sullivan reassured the veteran sergeant. Boyer's eyes were closing, and he was gasping for breath.

Mike Sullivan raised his voice. "God, you can't take this man. God, his family needs him—we need him!" Mike Sullivan had not been a regular churchgoer in years, and he wondered if God would be listening to his pleas, his prayer, from a part-time Catholic.

Officer Sullivan, still applying pressure on Sergeant Boyer's neck, at first did not hear the paramedic say, "Officer, I will take over. You did great."

Sullivan finally released the grip on his sergeant's bloody neck and quietly knelt by his sergeant's side. It was close to dusk now, and the orangish tone of the streetlights started to come to life. Everywhere, there were District One cars, uniformed officers standing about directing the hectic scene, police car radios humming with commands, and onlookers with their cell phones flashing, standing behind the yellow POLICE LINE DO NOT CROSS tape.

"Sullivan, Mike, you need to come with me." Lieutenant Adams lightly touched Mike's shoulder and handed him a bottle of water.

"Sergeant Boyer is headed to the hospital, and the crime scene is secure. Come with me. I will drive you back to the station, and we will get started on your report."

Sullivan nodded and got into his lieutenant's car, staring out the window, saying nothing, wondering if he had lost a sergeant, a friend.

CHAPTER 2:

Josiah

David opened his eyes and was quite disorientated, as nothing looked or felt familiar around him.

He was sitting alone with his back to a large oak tree on a hillside and a lush, green valley below him.

Where am I? thought David.

David slowly stood up. He felt OK—actually better than OK, as his whole body was refreshed and energized. He was wearing a light-brown robe reaching down to just below his ankle. His brown sandals looked old and worn but seemed very comfortable. He could not remember much of anything, other than being in pain, but now nothing hurt. David turned to his left as he heard soft footsteps in the brownish clay. A figure approached, dressed in a similar robe, this one light blue. He was tall and slender with dark features and dark, short hair.

"David, I am Josiah."

David looked at Josiah. He had dark, piercing eyes, yet his gaze seemed to radiate kindness and goodness that he could not look away from, and he did not want to look away. With confusion written all over his face, David simply stood there staring at Josiah, not saying a word.

"David, will you walk with me?" The tall stranger pointed down the path.

David followed Josiah. Nothing was said as they walked slowly for hundreds of steps leaving sandal imprints in the darkened clay after every stride. David saw jagged peaks off in the far distance, white, glistening snow on the top of each towering mountain. The path stretched on for some time as they trekked downward. Eventually, they leveled off and reached a wooded area. Tall, majestic pines rose up on both sides of a dirt path lined with thick needles.

David heard the crunching of Josiah's sandals walking a few feet in front of him. Josiah seems to be picking up the pace, so David did as well. Josiah, taller than David, walked with a long stride, a purposeful stride. The pines towering over the two travelers produced a unique and pleasant aroma, one that he had smelled before, perhaps when he was a boy. Several minutes later, as the walk between the pines continued, David remembered. He had been sitting on a small table in his mother's crowded well-organized kitchen. She had been baking cookies, and David had gotten to taste some of the batter while waiting for the first batch to finish baking. The smell made David smile.

The memory quickly faded as Josiah slowed down and turned, speaking softly. "David, you will enjoy this creation."

As they rounded a bend, a crystal, bright-blue lake appeared. It was the color of the sky, the ocean, icebergs, and robin eggs— it was breathtaking. Josiah motioned to David to sit on the small, sandy beach encircling the lake as they looked out over the mirror like water. A large, slender rainbow trout appeared a few inches above the surface and quickly disappeared. Across the small lake, David saw two small, brownish fawns balancing precariously on their scrawny legs, lowering their heads for a drink from the cool waters.

"The Father's work is beautiful; would you not agree?" said Josiah.

"Yes, it is so peaceful," replied David.

"David, I am glad that our Father brought you here so we could talk, so you can see the beauty of his creation, the glimpses of New Jerusalem and the New Earth that our Father has already prepared."

Josiah paused for a moment, looking out on the still water. "Paul told the faithful brothers and sisters of Christ in Colossae that 'all things have been created through him and for him.'"

Just then a massive eagle glided over the lake; its long wingspan almost hid the beautiful bird from view. David saw the powerful talons outstretched, skimming a few inches from the surface. Then suddenly, the eagle's feet submerged briefly in the sky-blue water and emerged quickly with its prey as it flew off toward the pines. A slight breeze picked up, and the fawns jumped gracefully back to the trees. Other brown trout seemed content to stay below the surface for now. A few puffy clouds appeared overhead, dotting the brilliant blue sky.

"I enjoy these waters here; it is a good place to rest and talk," Josiah said. "We have walked far today. Please try these." Josiah removed some bright red berries from a pouch hidden in his robe.

The berries were delicious—just the right amount of sweetness. They had walked a long way, yet, David was not tired. He felt energized, felt strong, felt like running. *Would Josiah want to run with him?* David thought.

"David, I am sorry to break you away from your thoughts," Josiah interjected. "It is a lovely place to think, to pray. Our Father has made such wonderful beauty." Josiah lowered his head and quietly thanked God for this day, this time with this man. Finishing his prayer, he looked at David, touching his shoulder.

"David, the Father loves you, and He has blessed you with many talents. He knows you love Him; He knows your faith in Him is true, and He is pleased. You will see the Father often on the New Earth, but for now, your upcoming journey is one that is special. I ask you to listen to remember our words together," Josiah said with a loving heart.

David said nothing as he listened to Josiah. He spoke slowly, soothing in tone but deliberate in his words. Josiah started to speak of men and their experiences from long ago—men named Abel, Enoch, Noah, Isaac, Jacob, Joseph, and Moses: godly men who were glorified for their faith.

"David, the word of old, the Torah—you know it well: you have prayed over it, you have read it often. Our Father has given you a great memory of people and of places. You remember the words of God's chosen people. Now it is time to hear your words," Josiah said. "God's beloved patriarch, Abram, or Abraham, proved his faithfulness, and Abram and his descendants were promised a new homeland. I would like you to tell me about Abram, the son of Terah."

David silently sat there for a moment, pondering what he should say and why. He was very happy here, whatever it was, and enjoyed walking and talking with Josiah. This place, this beautiful symphony of nature, was very new to him; it was so pleasing to his senses to see the amazing fields, valleys, lakes, and spectacular vistas. He remembered Josiah's words just a short while ago: "Our Father has made such wonderful beauty."

David bowed his head and prayed. "Father God, thank you for your wonderful and spectacular creation. Josiah has asked me to talk to him from your word, from Genesis. Provide me the words, the memory of your text. Thank you, Father." David concluded his prayer and looked at Josiah. Josiah's head was also bowed.

A light wind blew over both men, and Josiah looked up. "David, thank you for your prayer. Please tell me about Abram."

David nodded and proceeded. "It is written in the first book of God's word, Genesis from the Torah, that Terah, a descendent from Shem, Noah's son, became the father of Abram. Terah and his family, which included Abram's wife, Sarai, and Terah's grandson, Lot, left their home in the land of Ur. During the early part of their journey at Harran, Terah died. After that is when the Lord called out to Abram. Abram and his family went as the Lord had told him to the land of Canaan.

"Abram traveled to Shechem and Bethel, north of Jerusalem, and built altars to God at both places. Abram then went down to Egypt due to the famine in the Negev where he was staying.

"While in Egypt, Abram lied to Pharaoh about Sarai being his sister, even though she was Abram's wife. This deceit benefited Abram for a time as he acquired much livestock, donkeys, horses, camels, and servants. However, God was not pleased with this lie and sent diseases on Pharaoh and his household. Pharaoh, who had taken Sarai to be his wife, was made aware of Abram's lie and banished Abram, Sarai, and his family and possessions from his land. Abram then returned to the Negev in southern Canaan.

"God had blessed Abram along with his nephew, Lot, with much wealth: they had many livestock, flocks, herders, silver, and gold. The land where they stayed could not support both of their possessions as they were so great. In time, Abram's and Lot's herders quarreled over the land, so both men decided it was wise to separate. Lot chose the land toward the east, the plain of the Jordan toward Zoar. Abram chose to live in the land of Canaan near Hebron. After Lot had parted, God spoke to Abram, 'All the land that you see I will give to you and your offspring forever. I will make your offspring like the dust of the earth, so that if anyone could count the dust, then your offspring could be counted. Go, walk through the length and breadth of the land, for I am giving it to you.'"

David paused, and Josiah spoke, "Your memory of the word as written in Genesis is truthful and exact. It is pleasing to hear your words. Please, David, continue."

David proceeded to tell of how the word of the Lord came to Abram in a vision. How Abram, who was childless and his wife, Sarai, being old in years would have children.

God's word came to Abram, "A son who is your own flesh and blood will be your heir. Look up at the sky and count the stars—if indeed you can count them. So shall your offspring be."

David continued and spoke of how Abram, at eighty-six years old, had a son with the Egyptian slave, Hagar, and Abram gave the name Ishmael to his son. When Abram was ninety-nine years old, the Lord appeared to him and said,

"As for me, this is my covenant with you: You will be the father of many nations. No longer will you be called Abram; your name will be Abraham…I will establish my covenant between me and you and your descendants after you for the generations to come, to be your God and the God of your descendants after you. The whole land of Canaan, where you now reside as a foreigner, I will give as an everlasting possession to you and your descendants after you; and I will be their God."

God's destruction of Sodom and Gomorrah, Abraham and Sarah's involvement with King Abimelech, the birth of Abraham and Sarah's son, Isaac, and the sending away of Hager and Ishmael were all described in detail by David.

David's voice grew stronger, his words more profound, as he told of God's test of Abraham.

"God said, 'Take your son, your only son, whom you love—Isaac—and go to the region of Moriah. Sacrifice him there as a burnt offering on a mountain I will show you.'

"Abraham did as he was instructed and made a burnt offering, placed Isaac on the altar on top of the wood, and took the knife to slay his son.

"Just then, an angel of the Lord appeared to Abraham and called out to him, 'Do not lay a hand on the boy. Do not do anything to him. Now I know that you fear God, because you have not withheld from me your son, your only son.'

"Abraham saw a ram caught in a nearby thicket and sacrificed it as an offering instead of his son." David stopped talking, closed his eyes, and thanked God for His word and the ability to recite the scriptures as a blessing to his Father. He opened his eyes as he felt Josiah's strong hand on his shoulder.

"Your words of Abram, his life, his journey, are a blessing, David," Josiah said lovingly. "Our Father loves the faith and obedience in His children."

"You know the book of James, as it says, 'Abraham believed God, and it was credited to him as righteousness, and he was called God's friend.' You also are my friend, David."

David stood up and embraced his new friend. He looked out over the lake and walked a few paces in silence along the edge of the water. Everything seemed so serene; a wonderful calm and peace enveloped his spirit. The earlier confusion that he had experienced was no longer present. He thanked God, then heard Josiah speaking. "I am sorry, my friend. You may be tired, but we will walk again."

CHAPTER 3:

The Ride

Josiah and David walked in silence away from the lake along a narrow path that wound through tall, red maples. The colorful trees swayed back and forth in the breeze, releasing their brilliant scarlet and golden leaves in a slow-motion ballet, blanketing the trail as they walked. Josiah stopped as he noticed David admiring the leaves as they floated downward and lightly settled on the ground. He reminded his guest of how the apostle John had written about the leaves of another tree, the Tree of Life, in the Holy City of New Jerusalem. They were to be for the healing of the nations during another time. David nodded but was not sure he understood what Josiah had just spoken. They approached a small stream, gem blue in color, that curved through the trees.

"Let's stop here." Josiah and David sat on the shady bank near the water's edge.

"David, I want to share the *evangel*, the good news, with you. The blessed servant Paul, an educated Pharisee, later converted and wrote many beautiful letters to the people he lived with, visited, and preached to. He wrote from his spirit-filled heart, encouraging and instructing, among others, the people of Rome, Thessalonica, Colossae, Philippi, Ephesus, and Corinth. All who heard his message—traditional Jews, new Gentile believers, those who had no faith in God, Roman citizens, slaves—all were impacted by his words. Before his missionary journeys to spread the good news began, he was a sinful Pharisee, persecuting Christians. The Lord struck Paul down, blinding him by a light from heaven while traveling to Damascus. Paul was taken to the house of Judas, eating and drinking nothing for three days. Then our Lord Jesus came to a disciple named Ananias and said,

"Go! This man is my chosen instrument to proclaim my name to the Gentiles and their kings and to the people of Israel. I will show him how much he must suffer for my name." The Lord forgave Paul of his sins and restored his eyesight, setting in motion the greatest missionary journey of the ages.

"Paul's writing was always full of love and thanks to the people he met in his travels. Paul prayed constantly for these faithful brothers and sisters in Christ Jesus. He asked the Father to fill His children with knowledge and understanding that the Spirit gives so that they might live a life worthy of the Lord and please Him in every way, bearing fruit in every good work. David, this is a prayer that must remain in your heart and your spirit for all the time that you remain on present-day Earth.

"Abraham spoke to the wickedness and godlessness of ancient man and their darkened and foolish hearts, worshiping idols, and ignoring the Creator. Centuries later, Paul described how all men, Jews and Gentiles alike, are all under the power of sin. He quoted the scriptures: 'There is no one who does good, not even one.' Paul goes on to say, 'For all have sinned and fall short of the glory of God.' For the just payment or wages of sin is death. However, God our Father has blessed all men with a gift not earned or deserved, that of eternal life through Christ Jesus our Lord. 'For it is by grace you have been saved, though faith—and this is not from yourselves, it is the gift of God—not by works, so no one can boast.'"

Josiah paused, then looked intently at his friend. "David, you know these words, these scriptures. You have read them many times; however, the time has come for you to say these words to men and women who do not know the Lord Jesus."

Josiah looked over the babbling stream before them. All was quiet except for the water rippling over a few slightly exposed rocks. David also stared at the soft, soothing flow of the water. Josiah bent over and put his hand in the water and slowly brought it to his mouth.

"David, please enjoy the water." Josiah motioned to the riverbed. David also took a drink. The clear liquid was incredibly refreshing, soothing his throat.

Josiah stood and stretched briefly. "David, let's walk and follow the stream."

They both slowly strolled near the water's edge. Josiah picked up a few flat stones and tossed them in a straight, flat line skipping across the water, breaking the stillness of the surface.

"Your turn." Josiah flipped a stone to David. "Bend closer to the water. It helps."

David did as he was instructed, skimming the stone effortlessly, advancing a few more hops than Josiah's throw.

Josiah laughed. "You are a master skimmer, but I am not surprised."

They continued their walk along the stream with Josiah pointing out various birds chirping in the trees nearby.

"I want to share with you Paul's words to Timothy," Josiah said, his voice now firmer and stronger. "This is good and pleases God our Savior, who wants all people to be saved and to come to the knowledge of the truth. For there is one God and one mediator between God and mankind, the man Jesus Christ, who gave himself as a ransom for all people."

"David, our Lord Jesus has blessed you with a service, a purpose. Paul says that Christ Himself gave the apostles, the prophets, the evangelists, the pastors, and the teachers to equip his people for works of service so that the body of Christ may be built up."

"He spoke to the good people, the retired soldiers of Philippi, for it is God who works in you to will and to act in order to fulfill his good purpose. Your faith and your love for our Lord Jesus will be blessed. You spoke sincerely and true of Abraham earlier, and it was good."

Josiah went on. "The servant Paul spoke to the Galatians about faith: 'Understand, then, that those who have faith are children of Abraham.' So those who rely on faith are blessed along with Abraham the man of faith. David, you have great faith—you have that faith of Abraham. You are an heir to the father of nations as you belong to Christ."

Josiah's dark eyes locked with David's, but this time, there was a joyful glow to his gaze

"Your time here is almost over. However, there is something we will do before you leave."

Josiah led David up to a ridge overlooking a wide field of flowering golden grass. The slender grass bent as the wind whipped through it.

"See those large stallions near that lone oak tree?"

"Yes," David replied

"We must hurry before they leave; they get impatient and will not be there much longer. We must go!"

Josiah took off running, slowly at first, then after a few minutes, he increased his pace to a much more rapid run. David kept up, enjoying the run, just a few strides behind Josiah. As they neared the animals, David could see the small herd of both mares and stallions standing near the tall oak they had seen from the ridge above. The dark-brown oak's massive branches spread out significantly, providing shade for the herd. The mares were intent on grazing on the grasses beneath the huge trunk. The two larger stallions intuitively lifted their heads to the approaching footsteps. Josiah slowed down quite a distance from the horses and came to a stop.

"We should approach slowly and quietly," Josiah whispered.

The two most powerful-looking horses, their ears bent forward, watched intently as they neared. Josiah lightly stepped next to the coal-black stallion with the gray tail, lightly touching the forehead and muzzle of this amazing creature.

"Midnight, it has been a while, my old friend," Josiah whispered into the large black ear of the stallion. "We will ride fast today."

Midnight was relaxed, enjoying the light touch and soothing words from Josiah. He bent his large head and nudged Josiah's shoulder. Josiah slowly approached the other stallion, stroking his muscular frame and scratching his chestnut forehead.

"Sundance, you will be with David today. David, this is Sundance. You will ride him—you can trust him as he will trust you." A short, low-pitched whinny indicated the stallion approved of his new rider.

"Josiah, these horses—they are majestic." David said, admiring the bay and black coats of the mares and stallions before him.

"Yes, there are a blessed few who groom them with love and kindness," Josiah said. "Come, it is time to ride."

Josiah and David effortlessly mounted the stallions as Josiah whispered something in Midnight's large ear.

"They will know the way. Midnight will lead," said Josiah, and immediately, both stallions took off at a fast gallop. The other mares followed close by, letting the larger, older stallions lead the way.

David felt the cool breeze in his face and the warmth and power of Sundance's body beneath him. The exhilaration and freedom of riding this fast with Sundance, all four feet suspended momentarily and floating off the ground, was something joyous and exciting for the stallion's rider. The ride cut across a flat meadow, and the lead stallions increased their stride, running hard though the long grass. The riders leaned over, letting their faces touch the thick, coarse manes of their fast and powerful mounts. Midnight knew the meadow well and led the herd in a tight single-file formation. Sundance followed closely behind Midnight, his nostrils almost touching his fellow stallion's long, thick tail. As the meadow came to an end, several crimson-stoned buttes arose right before them. Midnight slowed his gait to a fast trot as they proceeded up a narrow rocky trail for quite a distance before finally reaching the top of the flat plateau.

The view was stunning as red and orange hues stretched over the horizon. The tall golden grasses of the meadow below continued their dance with the breeze. The mares and stallions were breathing hard, enjoying the break, sniffing each other with their flared nostrils. Midnight and Sundance faced their riders for a brief moment, lowering their heads as if to acknowledge, to thank Josiah for the honor to carry them through God's wonderful creation.

"Quite a ride," David panted

"Yes, the stallions are strong and fast; it was a privilege to be with them," Josiah responded.

Josiah looked over the valley below. "Brother David, it has been a wonderful blessing to be with you; however, our time together is over. I will pray now." Josiah bowed his head.

"Father God, we praise you for your wondrous creation. We thank you for this time with your beautiful creatures. Father, may you're loving and guiding spirit be with David. Continue to bring him wisdom and understanding of his journey ahead. May the name of our Lord Jesus be glorified through David and your word always be on his heart and the grace of the Lord Jesus be with him. In Christ Jesus, amen.

"We will ride once again when I see you…" Josiah hesitated, "…when you return."

The remaining mares glanced at David still upon Sundance, raised their heads, and nickered loudly. As if on cue, they darted down the butte. Suddenly, Sundance bolted back down the rocky path, trying to overtake them, surprising David.

"Whoa, whoa, Sundance."

CHAPTER 4:

"David, you're awake! Oh, thank you, God! How do you feel? Can I get you anything? Who's Sundance?" Rissa's excited voice exploded with joy and a multitude of questions.

David sluggishly turned his pounding head and saw his lovely wife leaning in for a kiss.

"Hi babe." David could barely get this out as his bandaged throat muffled his words. He tried again. "My throat really hurts, my chest hurts, everything hurts."

"David, don't talk for now. I am just so happy you are out of surgery and alive," Rissa said, tearing up.

David held his wife's warm hand and smiled at Rissa. "I love you. Can I have…" Talking hurt too much, so he just pointed to the water container by his side and made a slight drinking motion with his right hand.

"Water, of course, here you go. Drink slowly," Rissa said.

Rissa watched her husband take small slow sips. He had a large gauze on the right side of his face, and she could not see his neck as it was covered in bandages and dressings. She lightly touched his hair and kissed his check.

"David, if you don't mind, I will talk and you can just listen. Would that be OK?" David nodded, glad he did not have to speak, his throat just hurt too much.

"I don't know what you remember, but you were shot twice: once in the neck and once in the chest. You were chasing a young kid after he robbed Fiore's Jewelers. Mike got to you quickly and stopped some of the bleeding—he probably saved your life. Your vest protected your chest—so glad you wore it.

"Mike?" David whispered.

"Mike is fine. EMTs rushed you here, and you were in surgery for three hours. You lost a lot of blood, but the doctors say you will recover. You were lucky, David. No, you were blessed—God wanted you to live," Rissa said. "I want you to live. The girls want you to live." Rissa stopped as the tears trickled down her cheek.

David felt tears running down his face. He looked up at the lights over his head and closed his eyes again. He remembered running down the alley and seeing the flash of light, hearing the gunshots, and being knocked off his feet, hitting the pavement hard. He vaguely remembered Mike leaning over him, pressing on his neck, shouting at him.

Rissa's voice brought him back. "The girls are in the waiting room, but I think they are only allowing one family member right now in the ICU. I need to go out and tell the girls you are awake and talking, actually whispering."

David nodded and Rissa once again kissed his check, "Be right back. Don't go anywhere." She smiled and left quickly. An RN came through the door as Rissa was leaving.

"Sergeant Boyer, I am Denise. I will be your nurse tonight. How is your pain?"

David gave a weak thumbs-up and smiled. David was not totally being honest with Denise as he was trying to be the tough cop and cope with the intense pain.

"Let's check your vitals, and I am going to take a look at your dressing," Denise said, looking intently at his bandaged neck. "Let me go get some supplies—looks like your dressing needs to be changed." Denise left for a few seconds and quickly came back in. She checked his IV and his vitals. David's blood pressure was running high, but that was to be expected. Before she changed his dressing, she felt she needed to ask about his pain level again.

"Sergeant, really, how is your pain?"

"Not good," David murmured.

For the next several minutes, the experienced registered nurse proceeded to give the prescribed additional dose of morphine in his IV. She set up for David's dressing change as she took down the dressing,

"This site looks good; you were lucky, Sergeant."

David felt exhausted, but the pain meds were kicking in, so that was a relief. Rissa came back a few minutes later.

"David, the girls are so happy that you are awake. They all told me to tell you that they love you very much. I told them they might be able to see you tomorrow, OK?"

David smiled. He could feel himself fading.

"I'm really tired, babe. Can we say good night?"

"Of course. You get some more rest. I will be back in the morning." Rissa kissed his cheek. "I love you very much."

The "I love you" response never came as David's eyes grew heavy and then shut completely.

David looked over the serene blue lake, the one where the eagle had caught a fish not but a short distance from where he was sitting. Josiah was speaking, describing New Jerusalem and the New Earth. He spoke of how God will dwell among His people in His dwelling place. Josiah described the jasper-lined walls, the twelve gates made of pearls, and the streets made of gold. David was picturing all of this magnificence when he heard Denise say quietly, "Sergeant, I am sorry to wake you, but I need to draw your labs and check how your pain is doing."

David replied, "A lot of throbbing."

David glanced over at the digital clock. It displayed red numbers: 4:45 a.m. Denise finished her duties and returned quietly to the nurses' station. She stared at the computer screen, ready to document Sergeant Boyer's vitals. She looked over at her shift partner, Gloria, and exhaled. "He's a tough cop—I respect him so much. I am going to take care of him and get him out of here as soon as I can."

David was drowsy, but a few clear thoughts surfaced. *If he was in heaven talking to Josiah, why didn't God just keep him there? Perhaps it was just a dream, but it seemed so real. It had to be a dream or a vision—it was all pretty confusing. Horses—did he really ride a horse with Josiah in heaven? Why would he ride a horse? Other than spending that week on a dude ranch near Granby, Colorado, when the girls were still pretty young, he did not ride horses!* David was tired; he needed to sleep. He would figure this all out later. At 5:15 a.m., sleep once again overtook him.

Around midmorning, Rissa entered her husband's ICU room with one blue-hued rose in a square vase and a smile on her face. "David, you're awake! How are you feeling?"

"OK, tired," David responded sluggishly.

"I brought you your cell phone; a nurse in surgery got it for me. I am sure you got lots of texts and voicemails." Rissa set the phone on the little table next to the bed.

"Thanks. I need to get a hold of Mike and thank him and find out what happened," David said.

"Do me a favor: let's see what the doctors have to say and maybe take some more pain meds before you talk to him or any of the other guys."

"OK, promise. When do I get to see the girls?"

"I will bring them by tomorrow, early afternoon." Rissa smiled. "They want to see you, talk to you."

A light knock on the door interrupted their conversation. "Hello, Sergeant Boyer, Mrs. Boyer. I am Dr. Patel."

"Nice to meet you, Doctor." Clarissa extended her right hand.

Dr. Patel casually shook Clarissa's hand, then directed his attention to his patient. "Sergeant, I was the lead surgeon yesterday. How are you feeling today?"

"Been better," David said softly.

Dr. Patel began, "I want to tell you about your wounds and how your surgery went. You are a very lucky man, a very lucky police officer. One bullet passed through your right internal jugular vein and just narrowly missed your carotid artery, which could have been fatal. The emergency techs did a good job of pressure application at the shooting site to stop a lot of the hemorrhaging. We were able to repair the jugular vein, but you lost a fair amount of blood. Luckily, it appears you suffered only some surrounding muscle and soft tissue damage, but no nerve or any other significant damage. So, if no infection occurs in your neck, you should not have a very lengthy recovery. In addition, the body armor you were wearing protected you from a wound to the chest. You have no broken ribs, but you are significantly bruised, so you will have some pain there for a while, and your movement will be restricted for a few days. We need to keep you in here for a week or so to monitor your vitals, check on your sutures, change your dressing—things like that. I see the lobby has a significant number of police officers. I think you should limit your talking for a few days, so I suggest one of the captains or majors communicate to the department that you will not be seeing visitors for several days. Any questions I can answer?" Dr. Patel finished speaking and smiled at the Boyers.

"Yes, Doctor, will I be able to change the dressing when my husband gets home?" Rissa asked.

"Yes, the nurses will provide you with the supplies and show you how to do it," Dr. Patel said. "The staff here will give you all the required information to treat your husband at home. You can also hire a nurse to come in and..."

"No, that will not be necessary. I got this." Rissa looked at David with the most loving gaze. "I will be his nurse."

"You are in good hands here, Sergeant. I will have my team check in on you tomorrow. Take care." Dr. Patel excused himself and left the room.

David and Rissa held hands and just looked at one another. They said nothing for a few minutes, and then Rissa prayed,

"Father God, thank you for allowing David to live. My daughters and I need him as we are so blessed to have such a loving husband and father. Please provide David with a quick and healthy recovery. Provide him the strength and patience during his time at home and the wisdom when to return to work. Thank you for the wonderful care he is receiving from the hospital medical staff. We love you, Father, and I ask all these things in Jesus's name, amen."

The morphine drip allowed David to sleep that night. He dreamt of hiking with his family in the mountains, of running on a loose cinder track, and again of Josiah. Josiah smiled at him with his dark, loving eyes.

"David, you will remember all that we talked about. You will tell others of God's word and His loving grace and the free gift of His son, Jesus Christ."

His dreams started jumping all over the place, a few seconds here and there as a new vision appeared. He saw Josiah off in the distance, touching the mane of the black stallion. He saw a glorious eagle flying low over a glossy azure lake. Suddenly, the dream shifted. David found himself standing in a dark street, watching two men run toward him. As they got closer, he could see they were both young and armed.

David held his hand up. "Stop!" he shouted.

David awoke, sweat pouring from his hospital gown, his heart racing. He struggled to get out of the bed, pain rushing through his body. The IVs strapped to his arm stopped some of his momentum. The blaring noise of the bed alarm assaulted his senses.

Nurse Denise bolted in the room seconds later. "Sergeant, please lie back down." She touched his shoulder and gently pushed him back on the bed.

"They were running toward me," David said, breathing hard.

"It's OK. You are fine here—it was just a dream. Sergeant, I am going to give you a little Ativan so you will be able to rest for several more hours," Denise said calmly.

Denise administered the Ativan, and David was out in less than three minutes. She looked at the still-brave police officer lying in the bed and whispered under her breath, "You are safe here, Sergeant David Boyer."

David remained in the ICU for several days. There was no infection, and the swelling was going down. The pain was still intense, but the morphine was doing its job, allowing David to sit up at times and even go in a slow lap, IV bag by his side, around the unit. Rissa visited twice a day, and the Boyer girls got to see their father for a few minutes one day. Denise quickly became his favorite nurse as she changed his bandages and attended to him with the utmost care, adding some sarcastic wit that David loved. David was reading a long text that his daughters had sent when a visitor entered the room.

"Hello, Sergeant, may I come in?" said Lieutenant Colonel William Daniels.

"Yes, please come in," David replied, putting down his cell.

"I understand your visitors are limited now, but I know Dr. Patel, and he gave me permission to drop by for a few minutes. I just wanted to see how you are doing."

"I am improving, anxious to get home."

Daniels grabbed a chair and sat next to the hospital bed. William "Bull" Daniels was a big man, broad-shouldered with huge hands that gripped others in a tight vice at every handshake. Daniels had been in the department for twenty-eight years, and many projected him to be the next chief of police. Patrolman David Boyer had been on the force two years when Bull Daniels became his sergeant. Sergeant Daniels had taken a liking to his young officer and became an incredible mentor to David for the next six months. David had learned so much from his sergeant: how to patrol the streets, how to use a nightstick in certain situations, and, most importantly, how to interact with the citizens and people in the various neighborhoods. Daniels instilled in David to treat everyone with total respect.

"They often won't like you being there, but make sure they respect you and you respect them, always," his sergeant used to tell him.

In a job where language and communication were extremely important, David never heard Bull Daniels use a single word of profanity. His father was a Baptist pastor outside Jackson, Mississippi, and Daniels grew up in a rather strict Christian home.

"David, I want you to know that if you or your family need anything, the department will take care of it. You call or text me personally if you are not getting the assistance or help you need. You understand?" the lieutenant colonel said insistently.

"Thank you, sir."

"I would like to stay awhile longer, but Dr. Patel gave me strict orders that my visit was to be brief." The big man stood up, then bent over to kneel on one knee. "David, could we pray?"

"I would like that."

"Heavenly Father, my earthly father taught me at a young age you are a God of mercy, of compassion, of hope, of healing. Today, be with this brave sergeant and heal his wounds, provide him with quick recovery, and give him strength in his body and peace in his heart as he returns to his loving family. Fill his mind with wisdom on when to return to his job so he will continue to be an outstanding servant to his community. I ask all this in Jesus's name."

The lieutenant colonel got up and touched David's hand. "You will continue to be in my prayers, Sergeant." Then he turned and left the room.

David was touched very much by the visit. He reached over to text Rissa to tell her what just happened and did not see his phone. David was twisting his body at odd angles, thinking his cell was hidden in the bed covers, when Denise walked in.

"What do you think you are doing, Sergeant?"

"I can't find my cell; it was just here."

"I'll find it. You just lay back down."

Denise found the phone within seconds but decided her patient needed some scolding.

"How about I just keep this for the rest of the day and maybe return it after you learn to become a better patient?"

"Denise, you are awful." Both sergeant and nurse laughed.

"Sergeant, that is the first time I have seen you laugh since you have been here. I think you are going to be OK. I will tell Dr. Patel to release you soon."

David smiled again at his wonderful nurse. Perhaps she was right: he was going to be OK.

CHAPTER 5:

Katy Trail

David Boyer was in a good mood this morning. He had made chocolate-chip pancakes for his girls, and they had devoured every one that came off the old, black griddle. Rissa had gone back to work one week ago, and things were returning to normal. It had been two weeks since David had been released from Barnes Jewish Hospital. David was feeling so much better. His throat was healing nicely, though that large, crooked scar was a reminder of the seriousness of his injury. Today, he was going to spend a day with Sadie, just the two of them. He needed this time with his daughter. Actually, he needed more time for all of them. It wasn't that long ago when he was just getting home after that very tough time in intensive care.

Those first few days were crazy as officers and the media blew up his phone. He had told Rissa emphatically that he wanted Mike Sullivan to be his first and only visitor those first few days back home. Mike came over on his day off, a rainy chilly Tuesday morning. Mike brought bagels and Starbucks, and both men hugged each other like long-lost brothers reuniting after coming home from the war.

"Sarge, you look good. I can't tell you how good it is to see you."

"Mike, I apologize it has taken so long for us to talk since the shooting. I just needed some time to heal, to reflect, to be with the family," David said

"Are you kidding? I can't even begin to understand what you have been going through. Shoot, I would have probably taken immediate leave and hid out in Turks and Caicos for three months sipping on rum umbrella drinks if I had been shot." Mike snorted out loud.

"Mike, I have read very little since the shooting, and I have not taken many calls from the brass. Rissa has been doing a great job of screening them all, but I think I am ready to hear from you what happened that night," David said sincerely.

Officer Mike Sullivan proceeded to recount the details of that early evening, starting with the chase down the alley behind Fiore's.

"Sarge, if you remember, I was several yards ahead of you, and I turned right on South Grand to go after one of the suspects. He had a good lead on me, and I was thinking that I was going to lose him, crowded street and all. I needed our car or maybe the backups will start showing up. I'd decided to slow down and get on the radio when I heard two shots," Mike said, speed-talking to his sergeant.

"I sprinted back up Grand and saw you down in an alley off to the left. You were bleeding bad from the neck, gasping for air, so I put as much pressure as I could on your wound. I remember a couple of units pulled up, helping out where they could, and then the EMTs arrived and took over." Mike stopped for a second, trying to compose himself.

"It all happened really fast. I did what I could," Mike said quietly.

"Mike, you saved my life in that alley. If you hadn't come back, I probably would have bled out," David said, almost shouting at his fellow officer.

Both men said nothing for a minute or so, as talking all this through was tough.

"Mike, I heard the young guys that robbed Fiore's and shot me were caught?" David said, breaking the silence.

"Yeah, the next day, we got several tips, and after looking at the body cam footage, we were able to identify the two guys. They were both nineteen, and we found them in one of their aunts' apartments. They were both pretty scared, and the guy who shot you was a mess as he thought he'd killed a cop."

The two officers spent the next hour catching up what had been going on with the force, family, and NFL football.

David broke the ice to talk more personally to his friend. "Mike, how much longer are you on desk duty due to the shooting?"

"The department psychologist just cleared me yesterday—you know, the post-trauma review. Took a few days off this week—be back on the streets this weekend," Mike said.

"Good. Are you OK?" David wondered.

"Ready to roll, don't like shuffling papers," Mike said caustically. "Oh, by the way, we got a new desk guy: an older officer came over from the fourth, got a bad back, name's Elias something. You know him?"

"Elias…ah, not sure, kind of a weird name," David responded. "Mike, I am getting a little tired, so if you don't mind, I probably need to rest for a while."

"Sure, no problem, Sarge. It's been great to see you. Hope you recover quickly and get back to the job, OK?"

"That's the plan, Mike." David smiled, got up, and gave his fellow officer another hug.

David watched Mike Sullivan walk down the old stone porch steps and get into his white GMC Terrain. Suddenly, sadness came over David. He wanted to talk more but was fading back in the house those last few minutes. He missed the guys, missed the job, missed a lot of things. He thought of Josiah, and he missed him. Josiah had not been on his mind or his heart for several days, but now, out of nowhere, the time spent with Josiah came rushing back: the walks, the incredible beauty of where he was, listening to the calm voice of Josiah talk about the apostle Paul. Just then, his phone vibrated, jolting him out of those precious memories, Sadie was texting that she would be a little late as she was going over to her friend's house to study after school. He would get back to Josiah, but for now, he needed sleep.

Three days before David was scheduled to go back to work, he had a great day planned. Sadie, who was off school that day, had suggested they go for a hike on the Katy Trail in Saint Charles.

The Katy Trail State Park was a 250-mile stretch of crushed limestone and gravel that previously was the rail lines for the Missouri-Kansas-Texas (MKT) Railroad, better known as Katy. The Katy followed the Missouri River and wound through towering bluffs, wetlands, and gently rolling farm fields. After the pancake breakfast, father and daughter hit the road. They drove for about forty minutes before pulling into a trailhead, which was more like a dusty lot about a quarter of a mile off the road. The trail was a great place to run, bike, or just hang out with family for a leisurely hike. David and Rissa took the girls out here every few years for bike rides along the scenic historic trail. The best time for the Boyers to hit the trail was after a light snow. They all would bundle up, make their snow angels in the crisp white powder, and have their classic snowball fights. David remembered knocking down 5:30 mile repeats long ago on the smooth chat trail, while training for the academy.

It was a sunny day in mid-November that was cool, in the high 40s with almost no breeze. David had on hiking shorts, an old Cardinals sweatshirt, and his worn Merrells. Sadie wore an Under Armour hoodie and dark Lululemon leggings. They were both styling for their adventurous hike ahead. The fall colors had faded, and the trees were about bare of their leaves, leaving them scattered below their hiking shoes, covering the trail in many spots.

"Dad, do you miss running?"

"Yes, I do. It always provided me with peace, a place to go to when I needed to think, to work things out." They walked for about a mile before cutting off the main trail, following a tight path through the tall barren maples.

"Dad, I don't want to get all mushy, but we almost lost you," Sadie said, her hazel eyes misting up. "I know you would be in heaven, but we are not ready for that to happen. A girl at school lost her dad in a hunting accident recently, and she doesn't seem to be doing well. She's missed a lot of school, and I heard she is doing drugs."

"Sadie, c'mon now. That is truly sad about that girl and her father, but I am not going anywhere. I made it through this, and I will be there always for your mom, you, and your sisters. You believe that, don't you?" David said, grabbing his daughter's hand.

"Yes, I do," Sadie said. "I just want to say I love you, Dad."

Her father pulled her in close and hugged her tightly.

"You're the best. I love you too."

The hike continued on with father and daughter talking about swimming, school, and even boys. They laughed about all the goofy habits Staci and Jen had. They decided to race to a big broad oak right off the trail, about a quarter of a mile away. David gave Sadie a short lead, but he caught her and passed her right before the oak.

"You see, I still have some speed in these old legs." David laughed triumphantly.

As they got to the car and drank from their water bottles, Sadie stopped in mid-drink.

"Dad, Mom says you saw an angel before you woke up from surgery."

"Yeah, I have not had a chance to talk to you girls about that. Let's all sit down this weekend, and I will tell you what happened or what I dreamed, OK?"

"Sure, OK. Was he like Clarence from *It's a Wonderful Life?* " Sadie lightly jabbed her fist in her father's ribs.

"Funny," said David. "Get in, let's get back home. I can't wait to tell your sisters that I outran you."

The next day for dinner, David went and got two large sausage-and-pepperoni pizzas for the entire Boyer gang. They devoured both pizzas and topped it off with a carrot cake that Jennifer made.

"That cake was delicious, Jen. This was fun, guys," said David. "I know you got Netflix on the agenda, but before you do, I want to tell everyone about my dream experience."

The girls sat on the floor, and David started in on what he remembered. He told of waking up under a tree and meeting Josiah. He described Josiah and what they were both wearing. David tried to explain to his family how stunning the fields, the lakes, the streams were. He told how close he was to the eagle when he skimmed across the water. David grew silent for a moment, then proceeded to tell everyone some of their conversation and dialogue about Abraham, about Paul and his journeys and letters to the new Christians. He told of Josiah telling him that he will remember their discussion and he will tell others of it. He ended with the ride with the powerful horses and his stallion, Sundance.

David looked at his girls, at Rissa. "To be honest, I don't think this was a dream. I think this actually happened. I walked with an angel in what I think is heaven, and I am supposed to write or, I don't know, podcast about this incredible experience."

No one said anything for a few seconds, then the questions exploded out of all their mouths.

"Did you see Jesus?"

"Did you see people?"

"Is there snow in heaven?"

"You rode a horse, very cool! Was he fast?"

"How long were you there?"

"Was Josiah, you know, good-looking?"

"Did you tell Josiah about us?"

"Did you ask if Grandpa Ron was there?"

"Girls, girls!" David tried to stop all the noise and all the questions.

"David, when you awoke after surgery, the first thing you said was 'Whoa, Sundance.'" Rissa said calmly. "I thought you were dreaming of robbing a train with the Sundance Kid—you know, Robert Redford. I now know you're no train robber but a horse rider, a whisperer."

"That's cute, Rissa," David said, giving her a look like *I could use your help with the girls' questions here.*

"Your mother and I have talked about this a few times since I got home from the hospital, but not for long and definitely not in any kind of depth like I went into today. I wanted to get better, needed to get better, before I could try and sort this out and obviously tell you all what happened."

David went on, "So I need everyone to give me some time on this. I need to pray about this. I want the Holy Spirit's clarity and guidance going forward, and that may take time and will come with prayer. Until then, I am going to ask that we keep this discussion between the five of us, no one else. Can I have each of your word on this?"

Rissa, Staci, Jennifer, and Sadie all agreed.

The girls all hugged their father and left the room. Sadie stayed behind,

"Dad, I am so proud of you and glad that God used you—is going to use you to tell others about Jesus."

"Thank you, that means a lot to me." David again squeezed his daughter, wiping the tear with his sleeve that was slowly tumbling down his cheek.

After Sadie left, Rissa smiled at her husband. "I am proud of you too, David. I will pray with you whenever you want, and we will figure this out together."

"Thanks, babe, it's been a difficult several weeks. Could not have made it without your help and support. I go back to work next week, and you know I'll get back into the police life with all that entails, but this Josiah experience is not going away. It's on my mind and my spirit daily of late. I don't why God chose me, if God did indeed choose me to survive the shooting and possibly be a voice or something to others. If He did, I can't ignore it. I do know that."

Rissa and David hugged again. "I am going to join the girls and watch whatever Netflix show they choose, and we will talk later." Rissa left the room, and David went out on the back patio to pray.

"Heavenly Father, I am so thankful I am getting better. Thank you for my quick recovery and my wonderful loving family who is by my side. I am so confused right now, so I ask for wisdom and clarity in how to proceed in all this. I am reminded of your prophet Isaiah who through his vision heard God's voice, "Whom shall I send? And who will go for us?"

Isaiah responded, "Here am I, send me." I pray that I have that courage of Isaiah and will be a willing servant in what you ask of me. I ask all these things in Jesus's name, amen."

IT WAS EARLY MONDAY AFTERNOON ON A GLOOMY autumn day, and a light snow drifted through the Saint Louis area for a few hours. It was David's first day back after the shooting, and he decided to get to the precinct early. It was a good thing, as the snow began to stick on the streets, making the drive to work several minutes longer than usual. David was welcomed like a hero and celebrity as he made his way to his office. Dozens of handshakes and slaps on the back greeted him at every turn. There was even a large "Welcome Back, Sarge" poster signed by all the officers and brass sitting on his desk. His office had been cleaned and all papers stacked neatly in baskets on his old wooden desk. It was good to be back, but David knew tonight would be exhausting telling everyone he felt fine and catching up with the officers on what he missed since he had been gone.

Lieutenant Adams knocked on his door. "Sergeant Boyer, you look great. How are you feeling?"

"Good, I feel good. Got plenty of rest and ready to get back at it," Boyer responded.

"Don't push it these next few days. Let your training officers do as much as you feel comfortable. When you get a minute, go by and introduce yourself to the new guy, Officer Patros, at the processing desk. Good to have you back, David." Adams gave David a nod and then quickly left.

David had a thousand things to do this afternoon but decided it was best to meet the new transfer officer now before things got crazy, as his lieutenant had suggested. David walked across the large open office area and saw an older officer typing on his computer.

"Officer Patros, I am Sergeant Boyer. Welcome to the First District."

Patros stood up and extended his hand, "Elias Patros, nice to meet you. How are you feeling? Welcome back, by the way."

"I feel good, well rested. Good to be back," Sergeant Boyer replied. "So, you came over from the Fourth, and you're currently on limited light duty?"

"Yes, I hurt my back from a fall at home a few months ago. Getting better, but I thought it best to work at the station on restricted duty for a while," said Patros.

"We can surely use the help, so glad you're here," Boyer responded. "Got to prepare for the roll call. If there is anything you need, let me know."

Boyer walked back to his office, stopping for a minute to look out the window at the falling snow. It was still coming down, and it appeared they would get more than the forecast had predicted. Going to be some accidents tonight, Boyer thought. Hopefully, the good citizens will stay off the streets.

Boyer was back at his desk when Officer Patros stuck his head in the doorway. "Excuse me, Sarge, you have a minute?"

"C'mon in," Boyer said

"Nice-looking family," Patros commented, pointing to the family portrait on his sergeant's desk.

"Thank you, yeah, they are my pride and joy," Sergeant Boyer said with a proud smile. "You married? Kids?"

"I lost my wife recently from cancer, and I got a son in the navy."

"I am sorry, Elias; I did not know that," Boyer responded, feeling bad that he even brought up the whole family question.

"Yes, Sophia had brain cancer, pretty rough time, but she is in a good place now. She is probably taking care of horses, grooming them with the other angels."

"What did you say?" Sergeant Boyer said with a startle. "About the horses, I mean."

"Sophia loved horses. She had a fine mare that she took care of for years, at a stable near Pevely. So, I just figure that is what she is doing in heaven. Sarge, you are busy; we can talk later." Elias nodded, turned, and left the doorway.

David sat there stunned, trying to process what he had just heard from the new transfer, about Sophia grooming horses in heaven. He thought for a second, then remembered distinctly what Josiah had said before their ride:

"Yes, there are a blessed few who groom them with love and kindness."

David stood up and gazed out the window. Giant pointed white flakes danced through the air lightly touching down on the ground outside the building. He had a roll call in fifteen minutes, but he could not focus on that right now. He wanted to text Rissa to tell her about meeting Elias and the whole grooming horse thing but decided he would wait and talk with her in the morning. David continued to stare out the window, watching the parking lot, the streets becoming disguised in a white blanket. David remembered Jen asking the other night if there was snow in heaven.

David thought, *maybe next time, Josiah and I will go cross-country skiing.* David picked up his notebook and headed to roll call, smiling the entire way.

CHAPTER 6:

Boone

Rissa pulled into an open spot on the street not far from the Boyer residence on Devonshire. They had lived there for ten years, and she still loved her old, charming house. She did not get out of the car right away as she just wanted to sit and relax for a few minutes. It had been a long week, especially the last two days, as she was in lengthy meetings with her law firm's new client, preparing their responses to discovery by opposing counsel. The client, a single man in his late forties, was suing his former employer, a five-star luxury hotel in the downtown area, for wrongful termination. This guy was an odd duck with quirky body language and annoying comments throughout the meetings. Senior partner Randall Jennings was going to have his hands full with this case. Rissa was glad to be out of the office and just sitting in the car, listening to her soothing ambient music on Spotify. This was almost as good as the stress-relieving massages at Christy's, her favorite spa.

A young mom pushing a jogging stroller trotted by. Rissa smiled at her as the mom went by the parked car, and it brought back memories. She remembered using an old Baby Jogger after Staci could hold her head up. It was a lifesaver as she was able to get her runs in while not having to use a sitter. She was a new mom, loving it all—well, most of it. They were so young: David was a new cop and she was a recent Northwestern graduate trying to get an entry-level paralegal job. There was no such thing as virtual work back then. However, they made it work as David worked in the afternoons, so they avoided full-time day care. Rissa's first law firm was a terrible experience. It was a small, family-owned firm located in downtown Saint Louis where they treated new paralegals rudely and disrespectfully. She hung in there for three years, quitting abruptly after getting hired at the Jennings, Sapinski, and Phillips Law Group. This new firm was a godsend, closer to home, and the partners actually appreciated their paralegals. Fifteen years later, she was a senior paralegal with great benefits, working from home—how things have changed. The Baby Jogger mom and child were circling again as Rissa was exiting her silver Honda Accord.

"Love your Jogger. Keep it up," Rissa said, thumb in the air.

"Thanks."

Rissa was encouraged by the young runner and bounced up the steps. She grabbed the mail from the badly in-need-of-paint box attached to the brick veneer near the front door. Sadie had an afternoon volleyball match in about an hour, and Jennifer had swim practice at around 7:00 p.m. Once she entered the house, she knew there would be no rest and her afternoon and evening would be jam-packed. David was working tonight, finishing up his first week back since the shooting. He was off this weekend, and oddly enough, the girls' sports schedule was light tomorrow with just an early volleyball practice. Not sure what David had in mind for Saturday, but he would probably be exhausted, so no plans were made for now.

⁓◯

IT WAS ABOUT 7:45 P.M., AND RISSA WAS SITTING ON the hard stands of the South County Aquatic Center, watching Jen do laps and catching up on some work emails, when she saw David's text: *Hi, let's get away tomorrow and take a drive to Augusta and maybe stop in at a winery. Weather should be OK. Date?*

Sounds great, just what I need, Rissa replied quickly and enthusiastically.

On the way home after practice, Jen was usually quiet as she was often exhausted after swimming 200-meter repeats. However, tonight was different.

"Mom, Dad seems different since the—you know, the shooting," Jen said, looking at her mother.

"He has been through a lot, Jen," Rissa replied. "We need to be there for him, all of us. Different how?"

"He hardly ever talks police stuff anymore when he is around us. I haven't heard a good cop story in a long time. Last weekend, he was sitting out on the patio, and he was talking to himself— maybe praying, I don't know—but he was out there a long time," Jen said quietly.

"Praying is a good thing, isn't it?" Rissa smiled at her daughter.

"Yeah, it is." Jen looked out the window as they were entering their neighborhood. Rissa parked the car, and they both walked up the path in silence.

As they approached the stone steps, Jen touched her mom's arm. "Why don't you skip Sadie's practice tomorrow and you and Dad go somewhere, do something together?"

Rissa smiled. "You know, we just might do that. Thanks, Jen."

The next day, Rissa was up early and got in a light run around Francis Park. Even at 7:00 a.m., there were several runners circling the square park. It was a great place to run, with plenty of shade when it was hot and a sidewalk or wide-street option to do laps. Rissa remembered how she had challenged David to a two-lap race around the park two years ago. David had given her a sixty-second lead, and that proved too much as Rissa won by fifty or sixty feet. She had lifted her hands skyward, doing the Rocky dance, and never let her husband forget that stinging defeat. After a scrambled-egg breakfast for the girls and a quick shower, Rissa and David left midmorning for their Saturday getaway.

Rissa talked about work for a while as David seemed content to listen. When Rissa asked about David's first week back, he did not say much, other than it was just different.

"Different how?"

"Hard to describe, just different. Desire wasn't there—I was going through the motions a lot of the time. I would be writing reports, and then I would just stop and stare out the window," David explained. "I would often ask the officers to repeat what their question or situation was on the radio. It was kind of embarrassing, like I was senile. A couple of guys noticed and asked if I was OK. I would drift away and start thinking about my time with Josiah." David continued, "It's on my mind constantly. Rissa, what if what I dreamed, what I experienced, was real? I mean, one minute I am bleeding out in a dirty alley, then the next minute I am riding horses with an angel."

"You know, David, people who may have had similar experiences where they said they saw Jesus or spent time in heaven were confused or clouded for a long time after," Rissa said.

"Yeah, I know. I never paid much attention to that, never read any of the books they wrote. It's not that I don't believe them; I just never took interest in that, until now," David said.

David and Rissa were on Highway 94 now, driving the curving, scenic two-lane road that wound through western Saint Charles County. Even though the colorful leaves were just about gone from the towering trees that lined the road, the drive was still beautiful. They slowed down as they drove through Defiance, the small town that was the gateway to all the picturesque wineries close to the Missouri river and David's favorite, the Katy Trail. About a mile outside of Defiance, they slowed down by the Daniel Boone Judgment Tree.

David pulled off the highway and into a small gravel lot. They both got out and walked over to the memorial. There, they looked at a large elm not too far from where they were standing, representing an old, massive elm under which Daniel Boone had held court back in the early 1800s as an appointed judge of the area.

"Just think, 220 years ago, Daniel Boone stood nearby and made decisions on people's property, lives, and matters of the law," David said as he gazed out over the grassy Missouri field.

"I read where he often took his Bible with him on hunting expeditions. I can only imagine that Boone must have reached out to God for guidance throughout his iconic and amazing life."

Rissa listened to her husband talk about Daniel Boone. She knew David was a history nerd and his knowledge of all this stuff was cool, but he seemed very distant standing there looking at the memorial tree.

David stood staring at the open field, thinking about how God touches certain men with a purpose, when he heard Rissa saying,

"David, David, maybe it's time we go?"

"You're right," David replied, and they both got in the car and turned back on the highway.

"I did not know you were such a D. Boone groupie," Rissa chuckled.

"What, groupie? No, not at all. Just—I was standing there and I felt something. It was weird; it was like I was back there for a second, listening to Boone. He was sitting there under the tree on a stump or something, talking to a family about some legal problem, something about property. He spoke slowly and eloquently with a Kentucky drawl. I saw him get up and then pray with the family."

"OK, Mr. Boone, I just saw the sign for our winery. It's a half mile on the right," Rissa said, smiling.

They pulled into River View Winery, which had just opened fifteen minutes before. There were plenty of empty tables, and they found a small, wooden one with a wobbly leg. David suggested they stay put since it had such great views of the valley below, as well as some of the Missouri River. A few napkin shims under the leg, and all was good. It was sunny and cool, but with jackets, baseball caps, and an outdoor patio heater, sitting outside was comfortable. David ordered a bottle of Chardonnay, and they sat back, looked at the views, and had a great time talking, mainly about the girls. Their server, Kacey, came over and asked if they needed anything. Rissa said they were good. Kacey left, and Rissa noticed a few tats on the backs of her legs.

"Did I tell you Sadie wants to get a tattoo?"

"No, you did not. Why?"

"Not sure. I think she wants a Bible verse either on her arm or her back."

"What did you tell her?"

"That I would talk to you. I did not say she couldn't, just let's talk about it again."

"Well, to be honest, I am OK with it but would prefer it where it doesn't show—you know, back, shoulders, foot," David said.

"Let's talk to her tonight," Rissa replied. She looked at her husband; she was so glad things were returning to normal. Maybe they could take a little weekend trip soon, just the two of them, to the Ozarks, Nashville, Kansas City, somewhere.

"This is what we both needed today," Rissa said, clinking her husband's glass. "Thank you for this, babe."

"I agree," David replied.

The Boyers finished their wine and bottled waters and were about to pay when Rissa got a text.

"It's Jen. She wants to spend the night at Rebecca's. I said OK."

David laughed out loud. "Rebecca…that was Daniel Boone's wife's name." They both laughed and walked hand in hand to the car.

David stopped at the Roadhouse in Defiance as he wanted to grab some lunch and sit outside some more and enjoy the pleasant fall day. The Katy Trail was a few hundred feet from their table, and they watched the bikers, runners, and hikers go by. A father was pulling his two young daughters in a bike trailer, kicking up dust as he rode by. David thought he could sit right here for hours people-watching, enjoying his wife's company, and catching rays all in one. His life had changed so much since the shooting. He seemed more calm, more relaxed, not worrying so much about the job.

David suddenly shared something from his dream. "Rissa, did I tell you I ran with Josiah? It was incredible; I felt great. I was running hard, feeling free and fast. We ran to catch the horses as they were grazing below a big tree. Maybe heaven will have a few miles of the Katy Trail nested in it somewhere; that would be cool."

Rissa looked at her husband and smiled. "I never thought about running in heaven, but it would be incredible." Then she chuckled out loud.

"What?"

"I just thought of that cartoon—I think it was called the Far Side. It showed this guy with wings sitting alone on a cloud, and the caption said, 'I wish I'd brought a magazine.'"

"I remember that," David said. "It's what a lot of people sadly think heaven is like. I never saw magazines when I was with Josiah, so I think that cartoonist got it wrong!"

A little later after burgers, fries, and diet cokes, the Boyers were stuffed. They walked over to the trail entrance, and David kicked the chat with his feet. Two young runners darted by, surprising both of the Boyers. David grabbed Rissa's hand to get her out of harm's way for the next track stars. pounding the trail. He was about to say something but hesitated. They were almost to the car parked in the crowded gravel lot when David blurted out,

"I need to tell you something. I am thinking of going on family leave. I will figure out the best way to explain it and be as honest as I can with the department. I would think they will understand, post-shooting and all that."

"David, you know I will support that," Rissa replied. "What would you do?"

"I think I am going to write about my time with Josiah. I think God will provide me with some pretty vivid memories of that incredible experience. My conversations with Josiah were very spiritual, I guess the word is. Just describing the splendor, I saw, would make for an amazing book. I don't know, but maybe it can be a blessing for a few people so they could know about heaven, about Jesus," David said, looking at his wife. "I know I am not a writer, but I think I can do this. Maybe it would only take a month or so, then I would return to the job."

"I think it is a wonderful idea. I would be so proud of you. Just leave out the whole Daniel Boone spirit thing at the hanging tree." Rissa smirked.

"Judgment tree," David responded quickly, then for the second time that day, they laughed while walking hand in hand to the car.

CHAPTER 7:

Ashley

Sadie was not enjoying the long walk to the Cor Jesu Academy student parking lot as the wind was whipping the leaves and discarded paper everywhere. It was sunny and bright, but not warm at all: her fingers and face were feeling the brunt of the blustery gusts. Two tests tomorrow—one in history and one in chemistry—so Sadie knew tonight was booked solid with studying. She had her mom's car, which was quite unusual, as Rissa was working virtual today and surprised Sadie in the morning by giving her the keys as long as she came right home after school.

Sadie hit the unlock button on the fob and jumped in the driver's seat, turning the heated seat feature on to high. The Honda Accord technology started working as Sadie was warming up as she slowly pulled out of the lot. She turned the radio on, and the Message on Sirius XM was playing some Casting Crowns song in the background. Sadie smiled, thinking That's my mom, and went to change the station when she slammed on the brakes as a girl walked right in front of her mom's car.

The distracted girl hardly seemed to notice what had just occurred and did not look up until she heard a loud voice,

"Ashley, Ashley, are you OK?"

The wind was tossing her long curly hair in several directions as the tall, thin student turned her head and barely uttered, "Yeah, OK, I guess."

"Do you have a ride home?" asked Sadie.

"Yes, I mean no. I don't know. My mom is not coming. Something came up," Ashley mumbled.

"Get in—it's freezing. I will take you home," Sadie shouted above the wind. Ashley slid into the passenger seat of the Accord, backpack resting on her lap.

"You weren't going to walk home, were you?" asked Sadie.

"Maybe. I have done it before," Ashley responded.

"Well, not today, you're not." Sadie eased into traffic. "So where do you live?" Sadie said awkwardly.

"Off Flyer, not far from the park," Ashley said.

They both sat in silence for a few minutes. Sadie was not sure what to say. *Do I say I am sorry about her dad? Do I ask her about the rumors of her drug use?* She thought this was getting super awkward, so Sadie broke the silence. "I played youth soccer at that park by you. Tilles Park, right?"

"Yeah, it used to be a cool little park. Not so much anymore," Ashley responded sadly.

As they were nearing Ashley's street Sadie realized she had not changed the station. She reached over to press FM radio when Ashley suddenly said, "Can I turn this up?"

Sadie nodded, and her passenger turned up the volume.

"Beautiful, Beautiful" by Francesca Battistelli was playing, and Ashley seemed frozen by the song. She stared out the window, and Sadie could hear sniffles.

Francesca was singing the chorus:

"Like sunlight burning at midnight

"Making my life something so beautiful, beautiful

"Mercy reaching to save me

"All that I need

"You are so beautiful, beautiful."

"Please stop the car!" Ashley almost screamed it out.

"What?"

"Please stop."

Sadie stopped the car, and Ashley opened the door and quickly got out. The blustery wind came crashing in, seeking to disturb the warm passengers. Sadie watched as Ashley walked over to a nearby bench and seemed to collapse on it. Sadie could hear loud sobbing. Ashley's face was buried in her hands. Sadie turned off the car, tied her hoodie tight over her head, and walked over to Ashley.

The cold wind abated for a few seconds, warming Sadie up. "Ashley, are you OK? What happened?"

The crazy and cruel wind got reenergized and started doing its callous dance all around them. Ashley just kept crying, large tears streaming down her cheeks. Sadie did not know what to do, but she was freezing and getting quite mad.

"Ashley, please get in the car. We can talk there, where it's warm," Sadie pleaded.

Sadie, deciding tenderness was better than toughness, reached out and touched Ashley's hand. "It's OK!"

Ashley looked up at Sadie and grabbed her hand. Both girls got into the car, safe from the howling wind.

Sadie started the car and turned the heat up to high. She found some Kleenex and offered it to Ashley, who quickly wiped her face and eyes.

With somewhat dryer eyes, Ashley exploded in confession. "I am so lost. I am so pitiful. Nothing has been the same since Dad—since he died." Ashley looked mournfully at Sadie, her nose running again.

"I don't even know you. I heard about your dad; I hope he is OK. If he knew some of the stuff I have been doing lately and he saw me with you, he would…"

"Ashley, it's OK. Nobody is judging you," Sadie said, now wiping a tear from her eye. She reached down to grab a Kleenex and let out a small giggle.

"What's so funny?" Ashley said.

"Oh, it's my mom. She's so prepared—Kleenex, hand sanitizer, flashlights. She's probably got a Beretta in the glove department!"

"Really?" Ashley said, surprised.

"JK." Sadie smiled. Both girls looked at one another and let out a long overdue and relaxing laugh.

Sadie put the Accord in drive and decided there was going to be a change of plans. A few minutes later, she parked on her street, and they both went through the Boyers' front door.

"Mom, I'm home. We have a guest."

Rissa was in the kitchen clicking away on her laptop and looked up as the girls entered.

"Mom, this is Ashley. I gave her a ride and convinced her to try your hot chocolate," Sadie said, enroute to the pantry.

"Hello, Ashley."

"Hi, Mrs. Boyer."

Rissa looked out of the corner of her eye and could see Sadie giving her the look to leave the kitchen.

"How is Mr. Boyer?" Ashley asked.

"Doing much better, thank God. And thank you for asking." Rissa smiled.

Rissa seeing the flushed faces and out-of-control hair on the young girls, ignored her daughter's request to leave. "Ashley it appears you girls were running a 5K in the wind out there, so I would love to have you stay for dinner."

"I can't. I have to let my dog out and I have a paper to write, but thank you." Ashley said, sipping her hot chocolate.

"Some other time, then. You are always welcome for dinner."

"Mom, can I drive Ashley home?" Sadie said, cutting her mother off.

"Of course, Sadie. It was nice to meet you, Ashley," Rissa said warmly.

"Thank you, Mrs. Boyer."

A few last sips of the hot chocolate, and Sadie and Ashley braved the wind and got back in the car.

This time, the silence did not last one block. "That song, the beautiful song, what it is really saying?" wondered Ashley.

Sadie knew the song and most of the lyrics and proceeded to tell her that it says that God loves them and looks at them as His beautiful daughters.

"Did you learn that at church?"

"Yes, but also I learned a lot about God from my parents," Sadie said.

"I don't think God loves me right now. I don't even think He knows me," Ashley whispered.

"Ashley, God certainly loves you."

They pulled up to Ashley's house. Sadie could hear a dog barking inside.

"Hey, what are you doing this weekend? Want to catch a movie or something?" Pulling out her phone, she asked, "Can I get your number?"

"Let me think about it, and I will let you know. Thanks for the ride and hot chocolate." Ashley half smiled at Sadie, got out, and walked up the driveway.

Once Sadie saw Ashley was inside, she drove back home, contemplating the last hour or so. *That was crazy!* Sadness came over Sadie as she couldn't imagine what Ashley was going through. Back home, Rissa tried to question her daughter about Ashley and her day, but Sadie asked if they could talk about it later. Studying about the Civil War and the economic impact on the North and South, was not going well. She kept thinking about Ashley. She remembered how Ashley had said that God does not know who she was. Sadie picked up her iPhone and opened up the Bible App. She searched "God knows me."

She found Psalm 139:1: "You have searched me, Lord, and you know me."

Sadie closed her eyes. "Father, thank you for your word. Your word says you know us. You know Ashley, and you love her. Father, reach out to her tonight and provide her some peace and comfort. Open her heart that she will hear your word. Give me wisdom and understanding so that I may tell her some day of your love and grace when I see her next. In Jesus' name amen."

A COLD STEADY DRIZZLE HUNG OVER SAINT LOUIS on Thanksgiving morning. David had to work that afternoon, so Rissa got up early to prepare the turkey for a 2:00 p.m. dinner. Around 11:00 a.m., the girls started to drift into the kitchen to help with the sides and the baking of two pies: pumpkin and coconut cream. With four cooks and bakers in the kitchen, it was crowded, but the Boyer women made it work with good humor and a lot of taste-testing. Everyone was excited about having four days off, but the nasty forecast was putting a lot of outdoor plans on hold. Sadie was peeling potatoes, alone in her thoughts, ignoring the playful banter that was occurring on the other side of the kitchen. She thought about Ashley, wondering if her holiday was going to be lonely and sad. She contemplated reaching out to her today but remembered she did not have her cell number. Sadie set the peeler down and left the kitchen, walking past her dad's temporary office. He was reading a Joel Rosenberg novel and did not notice her standing in the doorway. She decided not to bother him and was headed upstairs to her room when she heard Jen's loud voice,

"Sadie, you going to finish the potatoes?"

Sadie changed directions, went back in the kitchen, and peeled the last few without saying a word. The baking of the pies was in full motion, so she snapped out of her funk and joined the merry bakers.

After a delicious dinner, the four Boyer women, cleaned up the kitchen, and debated the evening plans. Watching a movie on Prime or gaming were the top choices. Codenames was the selection, and the five-by-five grid of cards with random words were set up. The teams were Rissa and Sadie vs. Staci and Jen. After close to two hours had expired, the spymasters and field operatives were fading, and they called it a night.

At the First District station, things were fairly quiet. A few officers brought in cookies and store-bought pumpkin pie. A few calls here and there, but for the most part, most people were at home not needing law enforcement that early evening. Sergeant Boyer had enjoyed his Thanksgiving with the family and was reading an auto theft report when his radio came alive.

"Twenty-one eleven?" Dispatch queried.

"Twenty-one eleven," Boyer responded.

"Twenty-one twenty-eight, request a location to meet."

Boyer responded to Dispatch that he would meet his officer at Arsenal and Gurney a little before 7:00 p.m. Sergeant Boyer wondered what that was all about. Mike Bevins was twenty-one twenty-eight, a good officer three years on the force. He had never had any problems with him or his arrests or reports. Boyer finished up some paperwork and left the station at 6:45 p.m. to meet with his young officer. When he arrived, Bevins and his partner, Officer Tony Rawlins, were standing next to their patrol car. The street was empty as the neighborhood took little notice of two police vehicles pulled over.

"Evening, gentlemen," said Sergeant Boyer as he exited his car.

"Sergeant," both officers said in unison.

Bevins started the conversation, talking fast. He proceeded to tell his sergeant that about an hour ago, he and Rawlins got a call for a domestic disturbance at the 1100 block of Oleatha Avenue. A husband and his wife had had an argument outside their flat, and the neighbor had called the police. They pulled up and defused the situation; however, a very brief tussle occurred between Bevins and the husband. Officer Bevins explained it was kind of accidental, and he felt the guy did not want any trouble and was very remorseful for touching the officer. Both officers handled it well and did not press anything with the guy as both husband and wife went back inside quietly. Bevins and Rawlins got back in their car, and Bevins noticed his badge was missing. Both officers searched inside and out for the badge but could not locate it.

"So, Sarge, I felt I needed to contact you and tell you what happened."

"Glad you did, Mike," Boyer replied.

"I feel terrible," Bevins said quietly.

"Since I trust you guys know how to conduct a surrounding search for lost property, I have another suggestion."

"Yes sir?" said Bevins.

"I assume the wife was in the vicinity the entire time the WWE match took place?" Boyer asked sarcastically.

"Yes sir, she was close by, getting loud a few times, but she quieted down after we asked her to calm down."

"My suggestion is go back to their residence and ask both of them if they found an officer's badge."

Bevins and Rawlins looked at one another, then back to their superior, said yes sir, and jumped in their car. Boyer decided to follow just in case things got out of hand. Sitting in his departmental SUV, he watched the two officers go into the small brick building. Three minutes later, both men exited the flat and walked over to their sergeant's rolled-down window.

Officer Bevins pointed to the badge pinned to his jacket and smiled. "Just like you said, Sarge, she picked it up and kept it. She swore she was just keeping it until we contacted them, but we reprimanded her pretty good."

"So, you think this deserves a report?" quizzed Boyer. "Domestic disturbance, resisting arrest, possession of stolen property!"

"Sarge, I mean we defused the situation, and it is Thanksgiving and…"

"Get out of here." Sergeant Boyer glared at his young officers and then smiled.

"Yes sir." Both officers got in their vehicle and drove off quickly.

Bevins looked at his partner. "We got a break tonight. We owe him one."

"Yep, that was cool of Sarge," replied Rawlins.

As the young officers drove off, Sergeant Boyer sat there for another minute, thinking about the job. It was these kinds of interactions with his officers that he cherished. He knew he was meant to be a leader and would probably get promoted soon.

Lieutenant promotions were coming up in January, and David knew his chances were good that he would get one of them. Then captain, major—it was all there ahead of him if he worked hard and impressed his superiors. David pulled away from the curb, and it hit him. *Wait a minute—God might have a different plan for him: there had to be a purpose in meeting Josiah.* He wished that he could figure it out or it would become clearer. Just then his radio sounded off: "Twenty-one eleven."

Back to reality.

CHAPTER 8:

Elias

Elias Patros started his afternoon shift one hour early. He normally did not like to put in extra hours, but something was on his mind today, so he was anxious to get out of the house and to the station that day. Officer Patros had been on the force for fifteen years, moving to Saint Louis with his wife and young son in the early 2000s. Elias's grandfather, Stavros, had left Greece in the mid-1920s and settled in Staten Island, New York. Stavros was extremely fortunate to settle in New York at the time, as the 1924 Johnson-Reed Act severely limited the number of European immigrants to the United States. Elias barely knew his grandfather but remembered stories his father told of how Stavros Patros was a very skilled boxer; consequently, a rich promoter pulled some strings to get their family in the country. His grandfather was fortunate to worked security and bouncer-typed jobs during the Great Depression, mostly due to his talent with his fists. Perhaps a young Elias Patros had some enforcement in his blood, as he joined the NYPD in 1992. His career was going great, and he became a detective in four years. Things took a turn for the worse during an arrest in the Bronx: Detective Patros fell down some steep stairs, causing a slipped or herniated disc in the lower back. Elias recovered, but as he got older, it bothered him off and on. The recent fall at home aggravated his disc, and now he was on light duty.

Elias was sitting at his desk packaging prisoner property when his sergeant walked by.

"Afternoon, Sarge." Patros looked up from his desk, acknowledging Boyer.

"Good afternoon, Elias. You're early."

"Yes, just getting caught up on some stuff. How was your weekend?"

"It was good. Weather could have been better but I enjoyed the family time."

David wanted to stay and chat but had a lot of reports to review and decided to simply say "take care" as he walked to his office. David was still determined to go through with the family leave request that he and Rissa had talked about. He just did not know the time frame to initiate the conversation and make the subsequent request to his lieutenant. The rainy weather that they had over the weekend was changing to a cold front moving in tonight from the north. He was not sure if it would get below thirty-two degrees for potential snow or ice, but either way, the officers would be wanting to stay warm tonight and drinking lots of coffee.

That reminded David that last week, Elias had mentioned grabbing a coffee at their lunch break tonight, around 6:00 p.m. David had agreed, but he was a little hesitant as he did not know how to process his desk officer's comment when they first met, the comment on his late wife taking care of horses in heaven. Oh well, thought David, that subject will probably not be brought up tonight. The early evening was busy as reviewing the incomplete reports from his men was tedious and time-consuming. At 5:50 p.m., Elias texted him, asking if they were still on for coffee. Boyer texted back that he was still on and he would be ready in about ten minutes. Sergeant Boyer shut his laptop down, grabbed his jacket, and walked by Patros's desk.

"You ready, Elias?"

"Yes, sir." Both men exited the station.

Boyer, driving the department's Chevy Tahoe, drove the short five-minute drive to Lou's Coffee House, a small but comfortable little cafe that had sandwiches and great coffee. A lot of the officers stopped in, and Lou Venansco knew most of them by their first names. Venansco was a Vietnam vet who had done two tours and was known for his mechanic skills repairing busted-up Hueys, but his real forte was brewing coffee. Boyer and Patros entered the Coffee House to a relatively quiet surrounding. A few locals were here, but right now, they were the only police in the place.

"Good evening, Sergeant Boyer. you're looking good," said Lou, extending his firm right hand to David.

"Evening, Lou. This is Officer Patros," said David, introducing his new desk transfer. Both men shook hands and said, "Glad to meet you," and then Lou focused on their order.

"What will it be tonight, Sarge?" Lou said.

"Two black coffees. We will be over here." Boyer pointed to a corner table.

Boyer and Patros sat down, the sergeant taking the seat facing the front door. As they waited for their order, David started the conversation.

"How is your back doing?"

"Getting better every week. Doctor thinks another four weeks or so."

"Well, not sure of your plans, but we could use you at the desk for a while."

"Thanks. Let's see how I am doing in a few weeks, but to be honest, I might not want to go back to the streets, so maybe staying on might be a good option," Patros said.

Lou brought the coffees over with plenty of cream and sugar. "Are you guys eating tonight?"

"Thanks, Lou, but we got to get back in a few minutes, so we will have to pass," Sergeant Boyer said.

"Holler if you need anything." Lou nodded his head and departed quickly. Lou had the utmost respect for his police customers, but he also knew they were busy, and he did not want to have idle chit-chat with them unless they were off duty. The black coffee needed help, so Sergeant Boyer shook several sprinkles of sugar and a little cream into his cup and stirred it several times.

"How is your son?" asked Boyer. "His name is…?"

"Nicholas—Nick. He is good."

"Navy, right? What is he doing?"

"Nick is on the USS *George H. W. Bush*. He is an aviation boatswain's mate. He works the launch of the Boeing F-18s and the Sikorsky Seahawk helicopters. He is always busy, so we don't talk as much as I would like." Officer Patros said, looking down at his coffee.

Boyer said nothing in response, as he could see the sadness in his fellow officer's eyes. He thought of his girls and how it would be if they did not communicate much. He could only imagine the hurt. The two police officers sat there slowly sipping their brew. There was an awkward silence for several minutes.

"Elias, you wanted to grab some coffee, and I thought you had something on your mind. Am I right?" Boyer asked.

Officer Patros hesitated then began. "Sarge, we don't know each other that well. I have only spoken to you a half dozen times, yet I think there is something on your mind and your heart as of late. I can see it as you talk to the men, working in your office. You just—pardon the bluntness—you seem distant! It's really none of my business, but there is something there—I can feel it. To be honest, I think it's amazing you are back to work so soon after the shooting. I am sure there are many tough days." Elias stopped talking. "Sorry, Sarge, I am blabbering."

David looked at Elias and said nothing, but he knew that his new transfer had hit the nail on the head—but how could he know that? He wanted to confide in this man, but how could he? He did not know Elias, and besides, this whole Josiah and heaven experience was between God and him. In addition, the Boyer family had made their pact to not discuss this with any-one. David looked up and saw two officers from the Fifth come in. He recognized the sergeant, an older cop named Robinson, and both men nodded. David did not want to continue this discussion right now, so he looked at his watch and then at Elias.

"Everything's OK. Let's get back to the station."

"No problem, Sarge."

David paid the bill and told Lou to stay safe, and both men walked to the car in silence.

Finally, Elias broke the quiet, "I'm sorry Sarge, I was out of line back there. I…"

"It's OK, Elias. It's been stressful since the shooting, and yes, I have a lot on my mind, but I have faith in God, and He will see me through all this. Tell you what—why don't you come over Sunday night to my house? Rissa will make her delicious pot roast…"

David got interrupted by his radio: "Attention, all District 1 cars in the vicinity of 1400 block of Hampton. Burglary in progress. One white male armed with a handgun. Location: Shell station."

"Back at it," David exclaimed, jamming the car into drive and heading to the scene.

SATURDAY WAS A WORKDAY FOR BOTH DAVID AND Rissa. David worked the afternoon shift as always, while Rissa worked virtually. Most chores were put on hold; however, the girls did chip in and straightened up their rooms due to their mother's encouragement. Rissa had a quiet Saturday night as the girls were all gone with friends, so she got to relax and read the latest Jennie Allen book. Sunday arrived with a rumbling thunderstorm all morning, causing the Boyers to get soaked going from the car to the church entrance.

"I can't believe I forgot my umbrella," said Rissa, covering her head with her Bible. David said nothing, head down, walking fast to the main entrance. Christmas was only twenty days away, and the church looked spectacular with the white lighting and several green spruces behind the stage. The service was good as Pastor Brian preached on forgiveness, highlighting Psalm 103 and God's loving and compassionate attitude toward them.

"'As far as the east is from the west, so far has he removed our transgressions from us,'" Pastor Brian went on. "Our sins have been removed from us, as far as it is possible for us to imagine."

On the way home, David spoke openly to Rissa:

"I want you to know I have forgiven that young man that shot me. God will forgive him also if only he would reach out to God and ask His forgiveness, but I fear he will not hear God's word and find Jesus."

"There are prison ministries, David. Perhaps he will know God through one of these," Rissa replied.

"Perhaps," David said as he pulled into the street in front of their house. "Girls, don't forget we have a guest tonight for dinner."

"We remember, Dad," said Staci, and the three girls quickly exited the car.

"Rissa, I am not sure what to expect tonight other than he will be served a great dinner," said David. "There is something different about Elias. I can't put my finger on it, but I sense a caring soul."

"Yeah, you don't often have cops over for dinner. I look forward to meeting him," Rissa said with a smile.

At 6:00 p.m. sharp, Elias Patros rang the doorbell at the Boyer residence. David answered the door, invited Elias in, and introduced him to his family. The girls all said hello, and Staci even asked Elias a few questions about how it was to work for her dad. Elias was very complimentary in his words for his sergeant, telling the girls they have a good father.

"You should be here on game night if you think he is so cool. He's a bad loser," laughed Jen. Rissa had dinner ready, and they all sat down in the dining room and enjoyed the roast. There was a lot of small talk about sports, family, and Christmas coming. David and Elias did not speak of police work, and that made the conversation more relaxing. The girls volunteered to clean up, and David, Rissa, and Elias found comfortable chairs out by the patio. It was a nice, cool, starry night, and David turned on the portable heater.

"That was delicious, Rissa. I want to thank you both for the invitation. I don't get out much these days, so it was very much appreciated," Elias said.

"You're welcome, Elias," Rissa responded. "We try to make Sunday night family dinner night, as our schedules are pretty crazy."

"If you'll excuse me, I want to help the girls finish up. Enjoy your evening." Rissa got up and kissed her husband's cheek. The two men talked about the department, the job, the environment out there where the people viewed police from a negative perspective these days. David decided to shift the conversation.

"Elias, my family and I have been through a lot these last several weeks, and we leaned on God to give us strength and solace. We are doing a lot of leaning these days."

Elias spoke, "Sergeant, you're a good man. I could see that when I met you: I knew you were a man of faith. I also share your faith, your belief in Jesus. God's ways are often a mystery to us, and it is difficult to understand what He is telling us, where He is leading us. I pray daily that my son and I will become closer. I miss him. I am learning to hear God's voice more, trying hard to follow His path for me."

David gazed at his new friend and thought about when they first met and how Elias mentioned Sophia was probably grooming horses in heaven. Elias was right: God was putting this older officer with a bad back in his life right now. David exhaled and thought there was no better time to tell his story. David proceeded to tell Elias everything that he remembered after losing consciousness in that alley. He told of first meeting Josiah, of the beautiful places they walked and sat by. He spoke of their lengthy conversations of Abraham and Paul. He was especially vivid in telling the time spent riding the horses with Josiah. David went further, telling Elias how he thought he was supposed to tell others about his experience and write a book, as Josiah was adamant that David be a messenger of the good news.

"So, there it is. Quite a story, isn't it?" David smiled. Elias said nothing for several seconds. He got up from the chair and stretched his back, then sat back down.

"I agree it is quite an amazing story, but I believe it happened as you believe, it all occurred as you have described. God has allowed many believers over the centuries to see and experience small moments in heaven. God always has a purpose to these events. I believe God gave you a tremendous insight into what few have seen. You have been blessed with an amazing opportunity to witness to a world that needs to know God and to understand His forgiveness, grace, and love for all of us," Elias said.

"David, I would like to tell you something that I am not proud of, if I may?"

"Please, go ahead."

"Sophia's passing happened rather quickly after she was diagnosed with brain cancer. She started getting these severe migraines and had trouble walking, and her balance was off. It became unsafe for her to go visit her horse, and she struggled with that. She was only in hospice for two weeks, then she left us. I remember distinctly having a very tense discussion with the Lord. I asked Him why He took such a sweet angel from her son and I? I actually asked Him; didn't He have enough angels? I was angry for several months, stopped going to church, stopped praying, A few days later, I had an accident at the house and messed up my back. Figured God was punishing me for my lack of faith. After about three weeks, I was moving around OK and was hoping for some sort of light-duty assignment. Out of nowhere, your precinct had an opening for desk duty working for you. Well, you know the rest. That night, I asked for forgiveness for being such a selfish fool. I told God if He wanted Sophia, then I was OK with that, and I praised him for His grace and love. God has a plan to bring us together—not to catch criminals but something much more important. I don't know the details, but I feel I am supposed to help you, to guide you along a journey that you are about to take."

Elias stopped, and with a benevolent spirit asked if they could pray. David and Elias prayed together on the patio that night. Afterward, they went back to the kitchen where Elias thanked Rissa once again, wished them both a Merry Christmas, and left quietly.

David and Rissa sat at the kitchen table and David told his wife how God's Holy Spirit prompted him to tell someone outside the Boyer family about his experience with Josiah. David knew that God wanted him to trust Elias and that he would somehow help in his journey ahead.

"So that makes six of us who know about Josiah." Rissa smiled. "I am glad you felt comfortable sharing with Elias."

"I think we should have another believer's perspective outside of our family core on all this," said David.

David got up from the table and cut a small slice of the pumpkin pie they had bought for the dinner with Elias. He brought over two plates and forks.

"Let's have a small snack," David said. "Rissa, I decided that tomorrow I am going to request family leave for sixty days to start in a week. I will then begin writing about my experience with Josiah, and let's see how God will use this to further His kingdom."

"OK, David, let's do this. You've got my support and love every day," said Rissa. David and Rissa held hands and prayed. The Boyer family's lives were about to change forever.

CHAPTER 9:

Questions

Sadie was making her way through the crowded hallway at Cor Jesu Academy between classes when she saw Ashley coming her way. She looked upset and shuffled by without looking up. A week before, Sadie had searched for her on Instagram and sent a follow request and noticed it was still pending a week later. Sadie was disappointed as Ashley should have responded by now. That evening, Sadie decided to send Ashley a message.

Hey, Ashley, is everything OK? You seemed upset at school today.

Surprisingly, a minute later, Ashley responded.

Hey. Sorry, things are rough right now. My mom is struggling and hasn't been around much. I am worried about her, and I don't know what to do. After losing my dad, I cannot bear the thought of losing another parent. Don't mean to trouble you with this—I just have no one to talk to.

I am so sorry, Ashley. Is there anything I can do to help?

I don't know. I think my mom is drinking a lot, and I don't know how to get her the help she needs.

Can my mom help and maybe talk to her?

Thanks. Your mom seemed nice, but I don't know.

Could I at least mention it to my mom?

Yeah, I guess.

Let me talk to my mom tonight, and I will catch you at school tomorrow.

OK.

Both girls ended their Instagram messaging. Sadie was feeling sad for Ashley. What a mess—dad gone, mom not there much. She was thankful her parents were involved in her and her sisters' lives, giving them freedom to make mistakes but always there to help when needed. Tomorrow, she would fill her mom in and see if she could get involved.

STACI TEXTED JEN ON AN EARLY THURSDAY AFTERnoon to see if she wanted to grab a salad at the Greek restaurant near her university. Both girls' classes ended at 2:00 p.m. that day, so it made sense to catch up. They met at home, and Staci drove the twenty-minute drive to Clayton. Staci had received a scholarship in accounting at Fontbonne University in Clayton, Missouri. It was close to home, and it was a good fit for her, as she didn't want to be too far from home when starting her degree.

Jennifer was a senior still trying to decide where she would attend college. She, unlike her sister, wanted to go to school outside of Saint Louis. She was considering University of Missouri and Northwestern. She thought she might follow in her mother's footsteps and be a part of the legal profession, although she was unsure whether she wanted to pursue the challenging law degree.

Staci and Jen found a table near the back wall and ordered their favorite on the menu, the horiatiki salad. Both girls were tall with an athletic build that helped them significantly with their volleyball game. Jen was wrapping up her senior season, and she knew this might be her last year of competitive ball. Staci had a good high school career but did not play any more club volleyball.

"Do you miss playing?" Jen asked her sister.

"Not really. It was fun being around the girls and the play-offs were always a blast, but it's time to move on," Staci replied.

"Yeah, I am done once the season ends. Might start golfing," Jen said with a smirk.

"Golf—that's not you. Maybe in thirty years but not now: you're too competitive."

"Golf can be competitive, and you don't dive on a gym court to hit a golf ball." Jen laughed.

Their conversation got briefly interrupted as two young guys stopped by, one wearing a Fontbonne track hoodie.

"Hey, Staci."

"Hi, Jason. This is my sister Jen."

"Hi, Jen, nice to meet you. What are you guys doing here?" said Jason.

"Having a salad, catching up." Staci smiled.

"OK, won't bother you anymore. But don't forget—a bunch of us run on Saturday mornings. Meet at the track at 8:00 a.m."

"I might be out there. How far do you guys go again?"

"Six miles. No big deal, you can keep up," Jason said.

Jason said, "See you around," he grabbed a to-go drink, and left the restaurant.

"How do you know Jason?" asked Jen. "He's kind of cute."

"Had a stats class with him and ran with him and some of the track team once in a while. They are super-fast, so it's hard to keep up with them," Staci said.

The girls, still working on their big salads, talked about the holidays coming up and getting a break from school. Staci suggested making a trip to Columbia so Jen could see more of the college town, as she had only been there once. The conversation shifted to their dad and his heaven experience.

"Staci, have you ever thought if Dad's dream was real?"

Jen thought for a moment. "Yeah, I wondered that too. I don't know much about heaven. In all the years I've been in church and youth groups, I am not sure I have heard anyone describe heaven like Dad did. I mean, what he said—it's like here, like Earth, only prettier."

"How about the angel, Josiah? I mean, that's out there. Dad talked and walked with an angel!" Staci remarked.

"Rode horses with him too. How crazy is that?" Jen almost shouted at her sister. "Why would there be horses in heaven?"

"I know, right?! On the other hand, maybe it was only a vivid dream."

"Maybe, but Dad is different these days. No cool police stories anymore. It's like he is fixated on this heaven thing."

"Do you think he will ever go back to work full-time?"

"You got to remember he could have died from that shooting, so maybe that's why he is not talking about cop stuff now," replied Staci. "Yeah, he will be back. He likes being a police officer way too much."

The girls said nothing for a few minutes, paid their bill, and walked to Staci's car. Staci decided to drive by Forest Park to see if anyone was skating at the old Steinberg rink. They parked in the lot and walked up to the railing. There were about twenty people skating, mostly young kids slipping and falling on the ice with a parent in tow. The girls stayed a few more minutes watching the entertainment, laughing when the kids went down but watching them pop right up and continue skate-walking around the frozen ice.

"Do you remember when we were about nine or ten, we came to the park and Dad rented cross-country skis for all of us after we had a big snowfall?" Staci asked her sister.

"Yes, I do. I fell a lot and had trouble walking back up the hill," Jen giggled.

"We all had trouble, but it was fun," Staci added.

The girls sat on a bench nearby, and Staci looked at her sister.

"Do you mind if I ask another heaven question?"

"Sure."

"If Dad was so descriptive of what he saw, then why doesn't the Bible describe that? Why haven't smart theologians and pastors told us all this in their books or sermons?"

"Staci, I don't know. I got a C in theology last year. You do have a good question, though. You would have thought a lot of us now or people before us would have known about what Dad saw and experienced."

"Let's ask Dad when we think the time is right in the next few days, OK?" Staci commented to her younger sister.

"OK."

The girls left the park, having enjoyed their sister time. With the possibility of Jen going away to Mizzou next fall, Staci knew her time with her best friend would not be as much as it had been these last few years. They had gotten closer once they grew out of that young to mid- teenage awkward adolescence. Sadie, now sixteen, was just about out of that phase, so the girls knew she would be a closer part of the sisterhood any time now. Staci parked on the street a few blocks from the house, and they saw their dad's truck parked nearby.

They both looked at one another and laughed. "Let's do it, let's ask him."

David had been in court earlier that day, so he was not going to the station until 6:00 p.m. He was in the kitchen on the phone when the girls motioned if he had a minute. He held up his left hand to say *give me five minutes*. David was a little frustrated from the call as it was the attorney from his court case today. Apparently, they wanted David to appear in court next week again as there was a problem with one of the jurors. David finished his call and went to get a case of bottled water he had left in his truck.

"Shoot, the girls. Almost forgot about them," he said out loud and turned back toward the house, water in hand. When he got inside, he yelled for the girls. A minute later, Staci and Jen came downstairs and started the cross-examination. Staci and Jen took turns asking the questions that they did not have the answers to an hour ago. They asked their dad, why don't we know about the heaven that you saw? Why aren't the good writers and gifted pastors telling the world about the heaven you experienced?

Staci kept going: "Once you finish your story and it goes out to the world, if that is your wish, why would people believe it?"

"Staci, Jen, these are good and thoughtful questions. The Bible in Daniel, John, and Revelations has many passages and verses of what heaven is like. There have been several books over the years written by fine authors on their interpretation of heaven based on scripture. People can read these books as well as the Bible and choose what to believe, but there is no denying God has provided us with an image and essence of heaven."

David continued, "You also asked whether people who would read my potential story would believe it. That is such a great question—maybe the best question. My experience, although unbelievable and unimaginable to most, really happened. I truly believe that with all my heart. Trust me on this—I would never put our family through potential negative scrutiny or ridicule because of a book I wrote if this was not the truth, God's truth. Josiah had me recall the life of Abraham, and for several weeks after I recovered, I did not know why. He is an angel; he knows all about Abraham. He did not need to hear it from me. Now I know why. Abraham's faith inspired me to not lose sight of God's plan for me. It was to reinforce my faith in this story that I am going to write. God has faith in me to write this book, so I must trust Him to guide me through this process." David stopped and looked at Staci and Jen once again.

"I love you guys, Sadie, and your mom with all my heart. I guess I am asking you both to trust me."

"We do trust you, Dad," Staci replied, "so if writing this book is what you want to do, we are behind it 100 percent."

The girls gave their father a hug and left him alone sitting in the living room. David was proud of his daughters for having such creative questions and wanting to know more about heaven. Then it hit him: all the time he was with Josiah, he did not remember asking one question to his friend. *How can that be? I would think I would have been flooding Josiah with questions about everything, just like the girls have been doing. Josiah was so wise, and the discussions we had were indeed amazing.* David decided to get a quick walk in, so he headed to the park. The neighborhood park was bursting with dog walkers, runners, and a few older folks taking a stroll. A beautiful black lab with a shiny coat wanted a sniff of David, and he reached down to pet the friendly dog.

"Sorry, she doesn't normally stop during our walks," said the older women who was holding the leash.

"No worries. What's her name?"

"Lily."

"Well, Lily, it was nice to meet you. Have a good day, enjoy your walk."

David continued walking, enjoying the people-watching and stretching his legs. *He thought of all the girl's questions, they were so smart, so in tuned to what was happening around them. I would have never have thought to ask questions like that when I was their age. He thought of all his young officers and the countless questions they have every shift.* He smiled, *everyone had questions but him.*

CHAPTER 10:

Writing

Monday afternoon was overcast and cool as David drove into the precinct. The evening before, David had drafted up his family leave request on his personal laptop and emailed it to his Saint Louis Metropolitan Police Department email. David knew there was no turning back or changing his mind. He was putting his faith in his God. He had his family's support, and he had the support of his new friend, Elias.

David felt invigorated as he walked into the old police building and reached his office. He closed the door and opened his department email, quickly retrieving the email he had written the night before, and copied it to Lieutenant Adams's email address. Sergeant Boyer hit "send" and then sent his lieutenant a text that he wanted to see him to discuss an important matter. Thirty minutes later, Boyer was in Lieutenant Gerald Adams's office, explaining the leave he had requested.

"Sir, my family and I have gone through an emotional and difficult time since the shooting. I thought I could simply recover physically, and then I would jump back into my current duties. That has not happened, sir! I am requesting this family leave so I can focus on my family, focus on my mental and spiritual health." David stopped and waited for his senior officer to respond.

"Sergeant Boyer, I can only imagine how difficult this has been for you and your family. You are an integral part of our operations here at the First, and I would be lying if I said we will not suffer with you not here. I do, however, understand the ordeal you went through bravely doing your duty and the challenges that present themselves in a post-shooting recovery. So, I will approve this request under the condition that we talk again in person in thirty days after the start of your leave so we can both reevaluate your health and the status of this leave."

"Thank you, Lieutenant. As I stated in my email, I will finish out this week to ensure Sergeant Hendricks is properly updated on all my duties."

"Good. Hendricks knows your men and women. Get him up to speed," Adams responded. "Keep in touch, Sergeant Boyer. You have my number, so text or call whenever you need to talk."

Both men stood up and shook hands. As David was walking out, Adams stopped him. "Sergeant, Happy Holidays!"

"You too, Lieutenant. Merry Christmas."

David left his boss's office with very mixed emotions. He knew he was doing the right thing to step away, and his focus on family and his health was very important, but was it the main reason he was taking family leave? Back in his office, sitting at his desk reviewing robbery reports, David was struggling with his conversation with his boss. Should he have told him he needed time off to write a book about spending time in heaven with an angel? That would have gone well!

The afternoon shift got worse by the hour. Two patrolmen got injured when they got broadsided by a truck. Another officer discharged his weapon, accidently killing a dog, and the family was in an uproar. When David got home at 1:00 a.m., he was exhausted. The house was quiet as everyone was asleep, and David sat at the kitchen table, reflecting on his decision to take family leave. Maybe he should do his writing in the mornings and on his days off and continue working. He could cancel the family leave request tomorrow, and things would go back to normal. David decided to sleep on it and went upstairs to go to bed. As he lay awake, he quietly spoke to his father.

"Father God, I am confused; I am unsure on how to get this all started, and I am not sure whether to continue working. Why am I second-guessing my decision I made twenty-four hours ago? Please provide me the wisdom I need to start this journey. Provide me peace and understanding to do your will, even when doubts and roadblocks get in the way. I pray all of this in Jesus's name."

David awoke early the next day. No one in the house had gotten up yet. He decided to go for a run and was putting on his old Asics Gels on when his phone buzzed. It was Elias. That is weird, David thought. Elias had never texted him before—plus, it was 6:00 a.m.!

The text was short and direct: *Start writing! Elias.*

Super strange—a person he did not know well, who had never texted, almost sent a command to him to start writing. Elias did not know about the family leave request nor about David's indecision about taking off work.

David did not respond and headed out the door toward Francis Park. The park loop was already hosting several runners, and he settled in with an eight-minute-mile pace. His mind was clear, and it felt good to stretch out as he picked up his pace on the Eichelberger hill. David thought of the strange message he had received a few minutes ago. Why would Elias text this? He kept mulling this over in his mind. David finished his third lap around the park and did a cool-down jog the few blocks back home. When he got home, Jen and Staci were in the kitchen eating breakfast.

"Hi, Dad! You're up early!" Staci said.

"Morning, girls. Yeah, I went for a run. Is your mom up?"

"Not sure," Jen responded, never looking up from her phone.

David grabbed a Dasani from the fridge and grabbed his phone. He struggled with what to reply to Elias, and decided to not respond right away. Starting to write immediately would have to wait! David got to work early that afternoon as he and Sergeant Bryon Hendricks had lots of things to cover. Hendricks did not ask David anything about the leave and was focused on learning his fellow sergeant's routine. Finally, at around 7:00 p.m. that night, his interim replacement spoke up. "Sarge, none of my business, but I respect you taking some time off. Your family and health come first. You go recharge; we will take care of things here."

"Thanks, Bryon," David replied.

Sergeant Hendricks had to go on a call, so he excused himself, and David went back to his reports. He had forgotten about the early-morning Elias text, so he responded that he was ready to go. David leaned back in his chair and thought about how he was not preoccupied with the family-leave decision anymore. He had peace, and that told him that he had done the right thing and God had answered his prayer. David thought about Josiah and how he would be happy with his horse-riding and rock-skipping earthly friend. God was good.

The following week, David had set up a little writing area in their small den and began his story. He was using his five-year-old Dell laptop, which was probably way behind in all the upgrades, but Microsoft Word still was functioning, so he had what he needed for now. David's remarkable memory was functioning amazingly well, as he started typing, starting with the night of the shooting. He clarified a few things with Mike Sullivan, and then the words began to explode on the mini screen. Meeting and walking with Josiah, seeing the beauty around him—everything was being recorded as David vividly remembered it all. David was recollecting the time at the lake where he saw the eagle. He was describing it as if he was watching Nat Geo on the big flat-screen in the Boyer living room. The large bird's grace and sudden quickness swooping right above the water, snatching his prey with its sharp talons—it was majestic. David paused for a minute, thinking about what he had just written. He had been hard at it, remembering all the details, all the words spoken, then transferring those memories to the keyboard. This was all quite exhilarating, this new project; it was consuming David. Yet in many ways, it did not make sense. David was not a writer; he was a cop, a leader of other officers risking their lives in a dangerous profession. David, however, was committed and ground away on his old Dell. Five days later, almost three hundred pages of the time with Josiah was written. David was inspired and was typing twelve hours a day. It was crazy how it was all coming together.

Christmas Eve was very special for the Boyer family that year. David had recovered from a very serious neck wound a little more than two months ago, so the Boyers had a lot to be thankful for. After a 5:00 p.m. church service, the family enjoyed a delicious ham dinner. The opening of presents began after the dishes were cleaned and put away. The girls were so thankful for their gifts as their parents were super generous. They were so surprised to unwrap Microsoft Surface laptops, Apple noise-cancellation AirPods, and Jared sterling-silver bolo brackets. Staci thought it was so funny they did not receive clothes for the first time ever. Rissa remarked it was too stressful to buy clothes for them anymore; that was what their part-time jobs were for. Around midnight, the girls all went upstairs for bed, leaving David and Rissa alone sitting in front of the crackling fire.

"It was a great Christmas, babe," Rissa said. "I think the girls really liked their gifts."

"Yes, it was."

"I am so proud of you with your writing, the progress you have made. It was a great decision to take that leave."

"Thanks, Rissa. God has been faithful; it has been a wonderful journey. The inspiration has been nothing short of a miracle. I am excited to see how it comes to fruition," David remarked.

The first Monday evening of the new year, Elias had the day off, so David suggested Elias come over so he, Rissa, and Elias could do a first review of the draft David had produced. The three of them sat at the Boyer dining-room table with printed copies and yellow highlighters and went to work. For four hours, they read the story together, asking questions and suggesting a few changes here and there. Rissa and Elias were amazed at what David had written. His detail was remarkable, capturing the beauty of creation he had seen as well as the intimate conversations he had with Josiah.

Elias excused himself to go make a quick call, leaving Rissa and David alone for a few minutes. Rissa looked at her husband, and tears started pouring down her cheek.

"David, this is the most incredible thing I have ever read," Rissa said, wiping the tears from her eyes.

"Thank you, Rissa. God is blessing and inspiring me with these words," David replied.

When Elias returned, David explained to his writing team that in the last chapter, he wanted to create a transition for his readers. They needed to know that heaven was real, that God loved them and wanted all to spend eternity with the creator of the universe through His son, Jesus. They all agreed that the takeaway, the purpose, of the book is not only that a wounded cop experienced the beauty of heaven for a short time, but that only those that trust in Jesus Christ as their savior receive God's free gift of eternal salvation.

"I will go back to my trusty little Dell laptop and, with God's Holy Spirit's guidance, tie my experience to this good news. Josiah, in fact, talked of this while I was with him," David said emphatically.

It was getting late and everyone was tired, so they all hugged one another and broke for the evening. After Elias had left, Rissa and David relaxed at the kitchen table.

"David, have you thought about the publishing process for this book?"

"Yes and no. I have not given it a whole lot of thought, but I did talk with Pastor Brian the other day, and he said I should talk to our new associate pastor, Steve Littleton. Steve wrote a book a few years ago and may be helpful. I never expected to be this far along so soon. You are right: we need to start discussing the publishing options. Not tonight, though—I am beat."

David and Steve Littleton spoke that next day. Pastor Steve told David he had written a Christian fiction a few years back about two young believers caught up in a family struggle over good and evil. He told David that finding a professional literary agent that specializes in Christian fiction could take weeks, even months. He emphasized that an agent would be the conduit to a large, reputable publishing company. The pastor told David to contact the agent he had hired; his name was Peter Diaz.

David did not hesitate to reach out to Peter Diaz, and they spoke by phone late that afternoon. Peter had enjoyed working with the Saint Louis pastor and said he would be interested in reading David's manuscript when completed. He said once he received it, he would get to it as soon as he could, but his father was ill, so he was not sure how long it would take to review it. David understood and thanked him for potentially jumping into this new project so quickly, especially under the circumstances with his father. On Saturday, David emailed Peter the manuscript, although the last chapter was still a work in progress. He relaxed that night for the first time in weeks.

The following week, David and Lieutenant Gerald Adams met for lunch at a deli off Hampton Avenue, just as Adams had requested. They caught up with things going on in the First District, but the lieutenant was anxious to find out if his sergeant was returning to the job soon. Adams decided to press his sergeant and asked David when he could return, as the district was shorthanded, and he needed his sergeant back on the job. David had anticipated that this request was forthcoming, as he and Rissa had discussed this last night. He knew he had finished the draft and all the heavy lifting had been accomplished. David proceeded to tell his lieutenant he could return January twenty-seventh. Adams was delighted, appreciating his young sergeant's decision.

David wanted to return to the department and felt he could manage the stress. Writing all day was great and inspiring, but he knew he could not just sit around while the publishing process was in the works. Peter had told him it could take months before a publisher would review it.

A day later, Peter Diaz called and had good news. He was curious about David's story and read the manuscript. He told David that it was an amazing read and he would be glad to represent him as his literary agent. David was thrilled, and they both agreed to work out the details of the agent contract in a week or so. David knew God was opening doors on all this, so he thanked his Heavenly Father and texted Rissa with the news.

The next morning, around 7:00 a.m., Elias texted that he needed to meet with David right away. David agreed and set up a breakfast meeting at the Saint Louis Bread Company on Chippewa. Elias was already seated, drinking his coffee, when David arrived. David ordered a white chocolate mocha, no toppings: his preferred sugar-laden coffee. Elias started the conversation.

"David, you know my most pressing prayers are for my son and for you and your story? Well, this morning, Nick texted me to say hello and to see how I am doing. Out of nowhere, he contacts me, praise God for that. He then told me he has been invited to a wedding in Chicago for an old friend from the Naval Academy. He is updating me on his friend Jason Peters and his wife, Julie. You'll never guess where Julie works."

"Chicago PD." David grinned.

"No, no, she works as an associate editor at Tyndale House Publishers in western Chicago. Tynedale, David, published the Jerry Jenkins Left Behind series and all of Joel Rosenberg's books. They are one of the preeminent Christian publishing houses in the country." Elias was almost shouting, drawing some attention from the older couple sitting nearby.

"OK, where are you going with this?" David replied.

"I explained to Nick that I am doing some research on some Christian novels and would love to talk to Julie if that would be possible. I did not want to tell my son about the book, not just yet. Nick did not think it would be a problem, so he gave me Jason's contact info."

"Tyndale—that is a major publisher. I thought we would go smaller," David said.

"We go with whomever you want. You are the writer, David. However, with your permission, let me reach out to Julie?"

"Elias, this is a good time to bring you up to speed on Peter Diaz."

"Who?'

David detailed the conversation and agreement he had with Peter Diaz.

Elias said, "You know, you have worked so fast. We will need a publisher soon; why not Tyndale?"

"Rissa will find this so weird as we were just talking about a publisher the other night."

"David, I truly believe this is a God thing. The rapidity of your writing, and now the possibility of Tyndale," Elias said excitedly.

"God is with us, I agree. Please contact Peter, and you both reach out to Julie Peters. Tell Peter you are my biblical subject matter expert on staff." They both laughed and finished their coffees.

ELIAS WAS SO EXCITED THAT HE TOOK THE NIGHT off from the precinct desk and worked on prepping for his conversation with Peter and Tyndale. That evening, he texted Jason Peters and explained who he was and why he wanted to talk to his wife. Being a police officer must have had some weight as Jason responded an hour later, saying it was nice to talk to Nick's father, and provided his wife's cell number with no reservations. Jason even gave Elias the best times during the next few days in which to reach his wife. Elias then reached out to Peter Diaz and brought him up to speed. Peter was not at all bothered that his new client had his "staff man" pave the way for a call with Tyndale House.

Elias and Peter called Julie Peters at exactly 2:00 p.m. the next afternoon. Julie answered right away, said hello to both men on the call, and seemed pleased to talk to Mr. Patros. She talked about the upcoming wedding and how she and Jason were both looking forward to seeing Nick soon. Her husband always raved about his friend Nick and his academic accomplishments at the academy. Julie explained she only had about ten minutes before her next meeting, so she shifted gears quickly:

"So, Jason gave me a brief update on why you wanted to talk, but why don't you fill me in?"

Elias started with how he had met Sergeant David Boyer and summarized the shooting incident. Elias did not know Julie's faith or beliefs, so he talked at a high level about David's experiences in heaven with Josiah. It is David's desire to put his story into print, so that others maybe touched by this potential book and come to know God personally.

"David has completed ninety-five percent of his first draft, and I have reviewed the manuscript, and based on my experience, I feel there is a really good story here." Peter inserted himself in the conversation.

"If I understand the timeline, your client has basically written this book, or will complete this book in less than four weeks?" Julie said with a surprised tone in her voice.

"That is correct. He has been very inspired," Peter responded.

"That is incredibly fast, even for an experienced author. So, I am assuming you want Tyndale to review the manuscript and see if we have something here." Julie said.

"Yes, yes, that is exactly what we are looking for," Elias interjected.

"Gentlemen, Tyndale House's mission is to open God's word to as many as possible. We do this by publishing Bibles in many languages, nonfiction and fiction books, and eBooks, as well as children's books. We are one of the largest independently owned Christian publishers in the world. We only accept manuscripts through literary agents; as you can understand, we get requests to review and publish new authors' works by the thousands." Julie paused. "I'll tell you what I can do since Nick is so important to Jason. Mr. Diaz, please provide your resume on the titles and authors you have represented and send my assistant the completed manuscript. I cannot promise a timeline on when we will review this, but we will do what we can."

"That is wonderful, Julie. David and I are so grateful for your help," Elias said. Peter also thanked Julie for talking to them on such short notice.

"I have to prepare for my meeting. Very nice to talk to you both, and Elias, say hello to Nick for us," Julie said.

After the call, Elias Petros was thinking about his son, Nick. He was proud of him that he was serving his country. The troubled high school years were in the past. Elias smiled. Nick was a lot like his great-grandfather: hot-tempered and skilled with the fists. Nick had so little leave time, making it challenging to fly back to the Midwest, so Elias decided he would fly east and visit Nick near his base.

God is good, thought Elias.

CHAPTER 11:

Elias had sent a rather cryptic text to David that he had spoken to Tyndale and suggested they meet in person. David responded about an hour later, inviting Elias over around 7:30 p.m. That afternoon, Elias decided to text his son to thank him for clearing the way for his conversation with Julie and ask his son if he could visit for a few days. To his surprise, Nick's number lit up his phone!

"Nick, so glad you called," Elias said excitedly.

"Hey, Dad, I don't have much time, and the reception may be pretty lousy as I am on the flight deck now," Nick shouted.

"I understand, son. I just wanted to thank you for talking to Jason for me. I had a great conversation with Julia."

"You're welcome. Jason is a good dude; we could use him on the Avenger these days."

"We have some catching up to do, I was thinking about coming out to Norfolk…"

"Hey, Nick, I could use some help stowing the aircraft tie downs," yelled aircraft handling officer Seth Lee.

"Dad, I got to go. We will talk later," Nick shouted one more time and ended the call.

Elias was so thankful that they were talking again. He needed Nick in his life now and was going to make sure they were going to restart their relationship.

The Boyers were watching *Blue Bloods* when Elias rang the doorbell close to 8:00 p.m.

"Sorry I am late," Elias said. "Grocery store was very crowded, and there did not appear to be much help working. I bought chips and salsa."

"No problem, have a seat. Can I get you something to drink?" David asked.

"Water will be good, thank you." David went to the kitchen as Elias glanced at the TV. "Hello, Rissa, thanks for letting me interrupt your evening. I hope I did not miss the Reagans' dinnertime chat." Elias chuckled.

"You're good. I expect the dinner sequence in a few minutes," Rissa replied.

"OK, enough Reagan family talk. What's up, Elias?" David said, entering the room.

Elias proceeded to tell David and Rissa about the conversation with Julie at Tyndale. He told the couple the conversation could not have gone any better. Everyone was thankful and excited that things were progressing so rapidly. David communicated instructions to his team that while Tyndale reviewed the manuscript, they should do their homework on a potential publication contract and their negotiation options.

"I don't know Peter that well, but it does not hurt for us to do our due diligence," David said.

"Look at you with your big literary words, publication contract," Rissa joked.

"Been doing some research that's all," said David.

They all laughed, then David led them in a prayer of thanks. David and Elias walked out to the street together where Elias had parked.

"Elias this is an amazing journey, all of it, and I want to thank you for your support and for all you have done." David shook his friend's hand.

"Modern-day Timothy and Paul." Elias smiled. "Good night, Sergeant."

DAVID SAT IN HIS MAKESHIFT OFFICE, REREADING HIS last chapter. David thought this was going to be the toughest chapter, as he was wanting to tie in the Josiah experience with a message for his potential readers to understand who God was through their acceptance of Jesus as their personal savior. Many people struggled with not knowing who God was, not knowing about His unconditional *agape*, love to all. They got bogged down in trying to be good, trying to do good, but that was not how God's grace worked; it was a free gift not earned but given to those who asked forgiveness and asked for Christ in their lives. The last chapter flowed; it was easy to understand but powerful in its message. David remembered a Bible study years ago, as the leader, a former drug addict, told the group their job as believers is simply to just be the messengers, then God will convict the hearts of those who seek Him.

David was a simple messenger, a cop who loved God, a man who was bestowed a gift of seeing what God's creation looked like. God knew His plan for David long ago. David's legacy was already determined, and now he only had to accept it and let it happen. David's memory went back to riding Sundance. He had done nothing but hold the reins, and Sundance had done the rest, guiding him along all the paths.

THE LAST WEEK OF JANUARY, JULIE PETERS FROM Tyndale sent David, Elias, and Peter an exciting email. Julie was fast-tracking this process again as a favor to Nick Patros and had her assistant prioritize the review of the Boyer manuscript. The editors in her department had liked what they had read, although they suggested a few changes. They were not crazy about the whole riding horses in heaven part of the book, but that could be discussed. Julie suggested they come up to Tyndale's main offices in Carol Stream, a western suburb of Chicago, and meet in person to start negotiations. David and Elias agreed to meet with Tyndale on a Friday morning, January twenty-eighth. Peter Diaz was in California, as his father was not doing well, and wanted to be there as his father lived alone. David and Elias decided to proceed to Chicago without their agent. They chose to drive the five hours, as flying seemed unpredictable at this time of the year.

David picked up Elias on Thursday at 11:00 a.m. in his 2017 Ford F-150. He felt confident in his four-wheel-drive truck in case they ran into snow. The forecast for the drive to Chicago was cloudy with the high in the thirties. Some snow and potential ice was headed for Chicago, but in all probability, it wasn't going to hit until evening.

The early part of the drive on I-55 was relaxing as they talked about family and police business. David shifted the conversation to Chicago. Elias had only been there a few times, as he had no family in the area, and he did not follow sports that closely. David, however, had a history over the years of going to Wrigley to see the Cards vs. Cub battles. He told of how when he was a young boy, maybe four or five, his dad had taken him to his first game at Wrigley Field. It was a classic game between the two Midwest rivals as center fielder Willie McGee hit for the cycle. That was not good enough, since the Cubs' star second baseman, Ryne Sandberg, had hit two home runs late, and the Cubs had won in extra innings.

"I don't remember any of that," said David, "but my dad told me later it was the greatest game he had ever been to."

Eventually, discussions on the book came up as Elias boldly asked if David was going to take out the horse-riding section as Tyndale had suggested.

"No way," David remarked. "It was an integral part of the whole experience. You should have seen Josiah's eyes as we were with the horses; his entire body language changed. It's hard to describe. It was like he had been their trainer for years; it was a unique bonding that was incredible to see and be a part of."

David felt like sharing more, and Elias listened intently. "You know, Elias, I created an acknowledgment section at the end of the book—standard thing to do by us senior writers." David winked at his passenger and continued.

"I was looking at it the other day. It did not look right—I mean, there were hardly any acknowledgements. I thanked my family, you, the pastors, Mike Sullivan, Peter Diaz, and Julie Peters, and that was about it. I had hardly any references or research people to acknowledge. I barely used Google in my research. I did use the Bible to verify scriptures, things like that, but not a whole lot. I mean, the most important acknowledge-ment should be God's Holy Spirit. I guess what I am trying to say is all the words were inspired by our Creator. Now that is a wonderful thing—actually, the coolest thing—yet very surreal."

The Bloomington-Normal exit was coming up, and David saw billboards for Illinois State University, bringing back some memories of road trips when he was in his late teens. Light rain splattered the windshield, and David turned on the wipers.

"When I was writing, I would often think of the twelve young apostles. I tried to understand their environment, their mindset, when Jesus entered their lives—young Jewish men working to feed their families, coexisting with two challenging powerful forces: the Pharisees and the Roman soldiers. They knew the Hebrew scriptures, the Tanakh, fairly well but prob-ably did not go to synagogue every week but certainly observed Shabbat. Then Jesus calls them, and everything changed. They heard the Rabbi's teachings constantly and saw incredible mira-cles. They understood God from the Tanakh, maybe even feared Him a little, and now they were seeing God in the flesh. He, in many ways, was like them, looked like them, talked like them, ate like them. I am trying to convey, Elias, is for these twelve Jewish guys, there was little doubt about who God was and what their purpose was. How could they not tell others about Jesus after he ascended into heaven? So, in some way, I feel the same. I have no doubt who God is and what my purpose is. Does this make sense?"

"It makes perfect sense, David. That is why we are on this highway today," Elias replied.

As they passed Joliet, some light sleet began to fall, but neither man seemed to care as they talked about the title of the book.

"Rissa and I talked about this the other night. We short-listed *Josiah*, *These Truths*, *A Ride in Heaven*, and *Beautiful Creation*, among others. Hopefully, Julie and her team have some good ideas," David said, now paying closer attention to the roads. They took I-355 north near Bolingbrook as they were less than an hour from their hotel. The afternoon sky seemed so much lighter now as freezing rain started to hit the windshield.

"Forecasters way off on this stuff: they missed it by several hours," exclaimed David.

A small layer of glazed ice was forming on the highway, and traffic was slowing to about 25 mph. Neither man said anything, but both worried as conditions diminished by the minute.

"What do you think, Sarge? Should we find an exit and get off the highway?" Elias asked.

"Maybe, not sure. Let's go on for a few more miles," David said, his eyes laser-focused on the road.

Another slow and cautious mile passed as they saw the exit sign to Downers Grove. The highway here did not appear so icy, and some of the traffic had diminished.

"GPS says twenty minutes. I think we are good," David remarked.

David felt he could increase his speed, so he gradually got the F-150 up to 50 mph as they both relaxed a little, thinking they were past the worst of it. The Illinois Route 38 intersection was coming up when things suddenly turned bad. This section of the interstate was glazed over, black ice laying hidden as they crossed under the overpass.

The Ford truck started to slide, and David pumped the brakes, trying to steer into the slide, but that only caused the F-150 to fishtail. David was fighting for control of the wheel, but the vehicle was not obeying. The truck veered ninety degrees on the slick highway. David turned his head slightly left and was blinded by the headlights of an oncoming semi tractor-trailer. Both trucks were now sliding in a direct collision course toward each other.

"Hang on, we are going to get hit —" David yelled to his friend.

The semi tractor-trailer smashed into the Ford truck, lifting it in the air for a few seconds then driving the truck violently right into the concrete girder. Interstate 355 was closed for eight hours that late afternoon and evening. The freezing rain changed to snow, as several inches of accumulation resulted in slower ambulance services and accident removal operations.

The driver of the Coyote Logistics semi tractor-trailer was taken to the Advocate Good Samaritan Hospital in Downers Grove, Illinois, where he was admitted with nonfatal massive chest injuries. The two passengers in the Ford F-150, both identified as Saint Louis Police officers, David Boyer and Elias Patros, were pronounced dead at the scene of the accident.

RISSA BOYER WAS HELPING SADIE BOYER WITH AN English paper when she got the call from the Illinois State Police. Sergeant Angela Roberts knew this was going to be a very difficult call. Sergeant Roberts took her time and, as calmly as she could, informed Mrs. Boyer that her husband had died in a terrible collision on Interstate 355 in very bad icy conditions. The sergeant offered all her condolences she could muster and gave her the contact information for the morgue and the state police. The call lasted just under three minutes as Mrs. Boyer barely spoke and dropped her cell phone as the call ended.

Sergeant Roberts did not reach Nick Patros aboard the USS *George H. W. Bush* until the early morning of the next day to inform him of his father's death.

Julie Peters was confused as to why her potential new authors did not show up for their 9:00 a.m. meeting on Friday at Tyndale House Publishers, nor did they respond to her assistant's text and voice messages. Jason called his wife around eleven that morning to inform her of the tragic accident.

On Friday, Lieutenant Colonel William Daniels sent out a Saint Louis Metropolitan Police Department group email, informing the department of the loss of two of its officers in a tragic vehicle accident outside Chicago. There was no information communicated as to why the officers were in Chicago at the time of their deaths.

⌒⌒

RISSA WAS SITTING AT THE KITCHEN TABLE ON Sunday morning, staring at a chair across from her. David had sat in that chair just a few days ago as they talked about the book and brainstormed titles. David's book, his project, was so exciting and inspiring. He had been energized like she had not seen him since his early patrolman days. Rissa had been so proud of her husband, as she knew David was creating something special, something godly. Now, there was no excitement—only sorrow. Her precious daughters had lost a father, and she had lost an amazing husband. The girls were all upstairs sleeping; they needed their rest as the last few days had to have been the worst days of their lives.

So much crying, so much holding on to each other. Only Sadie asked, why did this happen? No one had an answer as they just held each other tightly. Rissa's phone buzzed, and she ignored the incoming text from Mike Sullivan.

Lieutenant Adams and another sergeant had come by yesterday to extend the department's sincere condolences, and honestly, she could not remember a single word they said.

Rissa looked at her phone to see what time it was and saw all the apps staring at her. Only one caught her eye: the YouVersion Bible App. Its reddish color encasing the Bible icon stared right at her. Rissa stared back at the icon, noticing for a second how red it was. Rissa thought, *looks like my eyes right now and my girls' eyes when they open them this morning*. Rissa kept looking at the red, thinking about how horribly David must have died, red blood everywhere. The thought of the blood was making her sick, then momentarily, a calm came over her as the Holy Spirit whispered, "Does not blood also represent your Savior's sacrifice for us?

Rissa, for the first time since she received the call from the state police, prayed. She closed her eyes and prayed for guidance and strength during these next several days, weeks, and months. She prayed for wisdom and the courage she would need for her daughters. She told God that she did not understand any of this but that she would try to lean on Jesus to take her burden away. She told her Heavenly Father that she loved him and thanked him for loving her. Rissa opened her eyes, and more tears came out. It was going to be another incredibly tough day.

CHAPTER 12:

Remembering

The day of the funerals for Sergeant David Boyer and Officer Elias Patros was sunny and cool. Oak Grove was a large nondenominational cemetery nestled in some rolling hills in South Saint Lous. Oak Grove was prepared for a large crowd and numerous police vehicles, as police officers' services required extra effort for the entire staff. Officer Patros did not have much family, so it was decided to hold services and burials for both men that day, albeit at different grave sites at Oak Grove. Officers wearing black armbands started arriving an hour before the service started. Dozens of flower bouquets, wreaths, and pedestals lined the roped-off area near the gravesite.

The Boyer and Patros deadly accident stunned the department. The First District was really struggling with grief as they couldn't believe they had lost a favorite sergeant as well as their older transfer. Mike Sullivan was extremely despondent, but he pulled it together and gave an emotional eulogy at the church. Mike spoke of admiration, friendship, and respect for his sergeant. Before breaking down for several seconds, he told the crowd of a few incidents while riding with Patrolman Boyer early in their careers that got the church laughing and crying at the same time. The funeral service ended, and the Saint Louis

Police Department provided an escort in front of the lead hearse of the eighty-car procession. At the Oak Grove gravesite, there were at least 200 police officers in their dress blues solemnly standing behind the Boyer family. Rissa Boyer and her three daughters sat in a front row on black folding chairs, heads down as Pastor Brian said a few closing words.

"David and Rissa Boyer became members of our church eight years ago," the tall lean pastor spoke slowly and reverently. "In that time, I had the privilege to know him as a dedicated police officer and friend. I look at these young women in front of me now, who are going through terrible sadness and pain, yet I need to tell them God is good. David's parents, sitting to my right, have just lost a son, yet I need to tell them God is good. The strong contingent of law enforcement standing in the back are here to honor and remember one of their fallen brethren, yet they need to hear God is good. David Boyer, some twenty years ago, made a decision to accept Jesus as his personal savior. This incredible gift from God enabled David to understand and know personally our Heavenly Father. It is a transformation like no other, and David knew he could live life to the fullest, knowing an eternity with Father God and His son, Jesus, awaited him someday. This is a tough day for all of us here today and will continue to be tough for many weeks and months after. We may question, in the midst of this sorrow, how good is God? The Bible says in Psalms, 'For the Lord is good and his love endures forever.' I urge you all to leave here today knowing that God is good all the time and His love will sustain us, now and forever."

The graveside service concluded with hugs and short condolences from the officers, family, and friends lasting an hour. A young lady in a black dress that seemed way too big on her came up to Sadie; it was Ashley. They both hugged, and Ashley said how sorry she was. Ashley knew all too well what it was like to lose a father.

"Both our dads are gone, and it sucks," Ashley said, wiping tears from her eyes.

"Yes, it does, Ashley. However, I am so glad you came. I will text you in a few days, OK? That is, if you promise to respond?" Sadie said, smiling. Ashley smiled also and assured her she would talk whenever Sadie was ready.

Rissa was emotionally drained and walked slowly to the car, holding her oldest daughter, Staci's, hand with Jen and Sadie right behind, also holding hands. Mike Sullivan insisted he drive the Boyers' car, and he slowly pulled away from the curb. The department had rented a hall to have a memorial luncheon for all who wanted to give their last respects to the two officers. These post-funeral gatherings were fine for the friends and family of the lost ones, but for the immediate family, they were extremely difficult. Rissa wanted her daughters close by for support as the multitude of well-wishers stopped by for short conversations throughout the long afternoon.

By 6:00 p.m., the Boyer family were driven back to their residence by Officer Sullivan. Mike knew they were all exhausted, wanting to be alone, so he gave then all loving hugs and told Rissa he would call in a day or so. Rissa thanked Mike for all his support the last several days, especially today. Mike drove away and it was just the four of them. The Boyers all went to the living room and collapsed on the sectional sofa.

"Mom, it was nice and respectful today," Jen said quietly.

"Yes, it was," Rissa replied.

After a few moments of silence, Sadie spoke: "Do you guys remember when we had that tough football game in the snow, and Dad threw the ball too hard and hit Staci in the face?' She was dripping blood in the snow, crying and screaming. Dad thought he could stop the bleeding by packing snow in her nose."

They all laughed, and Jen spoke up next. "I never told you guys this, but when Dad was teaching me to drive, I hit a parked car. I stopped the truck, and we got out to see the damage, and this guy came out of the house and started yelling. He was very upset, I was crying, and Dad was trying to make peace with this man. Finally, Dad pulled out his badge, and the guy shut up and started apologizing. He went in the house and brought out a beer for Dad and a Coke for me. His brother did body repair work and fixed Dad's truck for free. It was so cool to have a dad who is a cop—I mean, was a cop."

Jen stopped, looked at her mom and her sisters, and lost it. "This isn't fair. Dad was nothing but good to everyone, to us, and now he's gone. I hope his angel is happy that he has him, but I am not happy. I am sad—I am mad!" Jen shouted, tears streaming down her puffy red cheeks.

Rissa held her daughter close and said, "I know, I know, this is all so painful for all of us. I don't know about tomorrow or next week, but I do know I love you all very much and we will get through this together."

They all cried, wiped their tears, and cried again. They remembered vacation stories, favorite Christmases, birthday parties, and, of course, all the sports. The memories were somehow bringing some slight healing to the incredibly tough day. By midnight, they were all talked out, all cried out, and the girls said good night to their mom and went upstairs. Rissa sat alone. She was scared, she was hurting. She quietly talked to her Heavenly Father, asking for help, asking for solace. Eventually, fatigue overtook her, and she slept on the sofa that night.

The Boyer family somehow returned to school and to work. The girls took a break from sports and their part-time jobs. They ate dinner every night together and talked about getting out of town for a week, maybe to go skiing in Colorado or beaching it in the Caribbean.

A week and a half after the funeral, Rissa received an email from Julie Peters. She offered her sympathies and her apologies for not making the funeral. Her husband had reached out to Nick Patros, but he was not returning his calls. Julie ended the email by asking Rissa to call her when she had a few moments as she wanted to talk about the book, if and when Rissa would want to. Rissa was struggling with calling Julie back. She did not want to talk about the book, but she knew Julie had done David and Elias a great favor in reading it and considering it for publication. She thought more about it and felt she owed it to her husband to at least have a conversation with Julie.

Rissa emailed her back later that day, and they set up a time to talk the next afternoon. Julie again offered her sincere condolences at the start of the call. Rissa appreciated that and told her it had been a tough time these last few weeks for her and the girls.

"I can only imagine, Rissa," Julie replied. "If you don't mind, I would like to share a few things about your husband's literary work?"

"OK," Rissa said.

"My editor and I like what we read. We find the story very inspiring and, to be honest, very spiritual. Tyndale over the years has supported works such as this, as we think there is a tremendous need for this type of Christian literature. Rissa, I know you are busy and you have so much on your mind and heart right now. I guess I am asking if you would support a Zoom call with my editor, Brian, and myself next week?"

Rissa did not reply right away and actually asked Julie to give her a minute as she had to step away. Rissa put her cell down and looked out at the backyard. Memories of barbecues and practicing serves and dinks with the girls came flooding back. She did not know if she had the energy or even desire to jump into being the point person for this project. This was David's work; this was his story.

Rissa picked up the phone. "Julie, I have mixed emotions about this. However, I will agree to talk to you next week. I may have one of my daughters on the call also, if that will be OK."

"Certainly, we would welcome her to join the call. I will email you the details. Thank you so much, Rissa, and you take care of yourself and your daughters," Julie responded and hung up the phone.

Rissa was already second-guessing her decision but had committed, so she would make the best of it. That evening at dinner, Rissa informed the girls of the call she had had earlier. She asked for their opinion and also if any of them would want to be a part of the Zoom call next week. Before anyone could speak, Sadie blurted out,

"I want to! I will be on the call with you, Mom."

"Wow, that was quick," Rissa said.

Then Staci, Jen, and Sadie all gave their opinions. They all thought getting their dad's book published would be the right thing to do. Staci was not sure her mom had the time to get involved or was emotionally ready, so she suggested they hire a lawyer or agent or something. Jen agreed with her sister, while Sadie looked over at her mom and said, "We got this, Mom!"

"OK, it's settled: Sadie and I will take the call. Your father hired a literary agent last month, so I will reach out to him for his assistance." Rissa smiled at her daughters.

Rissa called Mike Sullivan a few days later and asked for a favor. She wanted to talk to Elias's son and did not know how to get ahold of Nick Patros, as he was on a carrier on duty. She had seen Nick at the funeral, and they had talked, but she hadn't gotten his contact info. Mike said he would handle it and have something for her by tomorrow. Mike came through, found a direct line to the captain of USS *George H. W. Bush*, and they set up a call with Boatswain's Mate Patros and Rissa on Saturday evening.

"Hello, Nick, this is Rissa Boyer."

"Mrs. Boyer, hello. Is everything OK?"

"Yes," Rissa replied. "I am sorry to bother you while you are on duty, but I need to ask you something."

"Sure, anything."

"Your dad and my husband, David, as you know, were working on a book. Did you know the storyline?"

"No, he didn't say much about it."

"It's a beautiful story of an experience my husband had while recovering from his shooting in the hospital. It was a dream, a vision of David being in heaven. Anyway, David wrote about it after he recovered from his wounds, and your dad helped, with research and moral support—stuff like that." Rissa continued: "The publishing company that they were going to see in Chicago reached out to me, and I think they want to start the process and publish the book. I would like to know if you want to be a part of all this, the potential negotiations, et cetera?"

"Mrs. Boyer, I am honored you asked, but that was your husband's work. You take care of it however you think best. I don't need to be a part of that. Let me know how it all turns out," Nick replied.

"Thank you, Nick. Oh, by the way, what is the best way to contact you, other than from your captain's quarters?"

Nick laughed then gave Rissa his cell number, as well as a specific code to type in so he would know to respond. Nick was not taking a lot of calls these days, sorting out the death of his father and his own future. Nick thanked his captain who was standing outside his quarters and walked up to the flight deck.

It was a starry night in Norfolk, and Nick thought he saw a shooting star blast across the sky.

He had no parents now, no family—just the Navy. The USS *George H. W. Bush*, the final Nimitz-class supercarrier, was headed out of port in a few days for a training mission in the Mediterranean. Nick was glad they were going out to sea again—things seemed in order when they were at sea. Nick thought about the few conversations he had had with his dad the last month before the accident. His dad had seemed so happy they were talking again. He recalled a quick conversation when he was on the flight deck. He thought he remembered his dad saying something about coming out to Virginia.

Another conversation in particular came to mind. His dad had spoken of Jesus like he knew Him personally, like He was alive, real, and not some faraway rabbi from two thousand years ago. He had asked his son for a favor, to take some time and read the book of John from the Bible. *Maybe tomorrow*, Nick thought, *I will go ask the chaplain if he has a Bible*. Another star shot across the moonlit sky as Nick went below.

CHAPTER 13:

Even though Rissa was back working virtually from her kitchen table, she was still grieving a lot. She cut her hours to twenty a week, and her firm was giving her all the support she could ask for. She was getting inundated with emails, texts, and voicemails from her caring friends and family. She appreciated their concerns and checking in on her, but it was just too much to respond to everyone. She focused on her girls and a few close friends like Mike Sullivan and Laura Weathers, a dear friend from church. Laura had sent her a beautiful bouquet of bright yellow lilies along with the most touching card. Laura hand-wrote eloquently how much Rissa and her daughters were in her prayers daily.

She then went on to say, "God pursues us, He is with you, for you, every moment during this trying time."

She shared Psalm 23:6: "Your beauty and love chase after me every day of my life." Laura closed her short message to her dear and grief-stricken friend that God is after her heart right now!

The flowers and the card meant everything to Rissa. She knew God loved her and was out there, but she did not realize His ever-loving pursuit of her. Rissa put a note on her phone to schedule lunch with Laura that week.

That afternoon, her laptop notified her of an incoming email from Julie Peters with several attachments. Rissa hesitated for an hour before opening the email. She knew once she did, it was game on, and she could not go back on her commitment to continue seeing this through and ensuring people knew her husband's story. Rissa opened the email at 4:02 p.m. and started reading. The Zoom call was scheduled for 4:30 p.m. CST on Friday. Rissa had indicated a late-afternoon call would work best so Sadie could make it after school.

Julie and her assistant did a great job of creating an agenda for the meeting as well as providing a synopsis of each agenda item. Julie noted in the initial paragraph of the email that although Tyndale had already received a draft manuscript from Mr. Patros, due to the tragic circumstances, Rissa could have time to edit the copy and provide an updated manuscript if she desired.

The agenda was as follows:
Introductions
Discuss goal of the author and the book
Negotiation
Concessions clauses
Grant of right clause
Copyright
Subsidiary rights
Editing clauses
Terms of agreement
Advances and advance clauses
Consultation clause

Pricing

Marketing and advertising

Next actions

Although this may have seemed overwhelming, especially to someone that had never done this before, Rissa's experience as a senior paralegal had prepared her for these potential challenging discussions and negotiations. Rissa had done her homework on all of these agenda items and knew most of the questions to ask. In addition, she asked her senior legal attorney at the firm, John Phillips, to sit in on the Zoom call.

Rissa made spaghetti for the girls that evening, and they talked about the call on Friday. Rissa explained this was the first step in completing their dad's project, and although it was exciting to see how this all would play out, it might cause stress in their lives and resurface many difficult emotions for all of them.

Sadie was the first to speak. "Mom, I think Dad would be proud of all of us for continuing his story. Not to be goofy, but I think his angel, Josiah, would be proud of us too." The sisters agreed, and Rissa said she would order pizza on Friday night so they all could talk about how the Zoom call went.

John Phillips, the firm's senior legal attorney, suggested that he meet in person with Rissa and her daughter during the Zoom call. He showed up at 3:30 p.m. to review the agenda and Rissa's position on many of the clauses and options. Peter Diaz could not join the call as he was focused on finding potential hospice care for his dying father. Sadie got home at 4:15, changed out of her school uniform, and met the team in the Boyers' dining room with five minutes to spare.

"John, I want to share something with you before the call starts," Rissa started. "My family and I believe in what we are about to do here. We want to carry on David's work; it means a lot to all of us. Although I have no idea if the book will get published or what kind of success it will be, I truly hope people will be touched and inspired by it. What I am torn about is how much the publishers or marketing folks will use David's death and his earlier shooting incident to promote this story. I am not sure we can avoid that to some degree, but I don't want that to be a marketing tool. My family and I don't need that—we don't want that."

"I completely understand, Rissa. We will ensure contract provisions state you have full review and acceptance on all marketing, advertising, and promotional events," John remarked.

"Thank you, John. We can get into that later."

The Zoom call started right on time and lasted ninety minutes. All the agenda items were covered by the Tyndale's representatives. Rissa waived the right to edit the original manuscript as she said she totally trusted what David had written. A more than generous advance was agreed upon based on the price of comparable Christian fiction books in the last five years. Both parties agreed to a publishing timeline, and Rissa agreed to a consultation clause that Tyndale would design the jacket and cover, and even suggest a title with all to be approved by Rissa Boyer. As the call was about to end, Julie asked if Sadie had any questions. Sadie had been listening intently but was silent the entire time, letting the adults do their thing.

Sadie thanked Julie and her team for their time, hesitated, then spoke: "I know my dad is in heaven as we speak today. If people in heaven can be proud, then he would be so proud of his wife and his daughters. Dad, this is for you."

Rissa clutched her daughter's hand and thanked everyone, and the call ended. She then burst into tears.

TWO MONTHS LATER…

Tyndale House did a remarkable job of completing much of the publication process in such an inconceivably short time. They worked jointly with Rissa and per her instructions on the various clauses and provisions of the contract. The time came for Rissa to review the suggested marketing and promotional strategies and events that the Tyndale team had developed. Rissa did not want to create a blog or host a weekly podcast. She did agree that Tyndale could send out promotional emails and new-release notices through their website. Julie and Rissa had a long conversation about this limited advertising of the book. Rissa was adamant that the promotion of David's work be low-key.

"Rissa, I respect your thoughts on this, but can I ask why?" Julie asked.

"I understand your marketing approach, I really do. However, the girls and I talked about this in length, and we feel that God will direct this as He desires. We don't want notoriety through this story; we only want to complete David's wishes of writing about this incredible experience. If only a few people read David's work and it results in them finding the Savior Jesus because of this book, so be it."

Julie did not push the subject anymore, for now. She informed Rissa there were a few minor details to work out and that the official publication date would be in approximately three weeks. *A Window into Heaven* was published on May ninth and went on sale the next day.

Laura called that day and told Rissa how proud she was of her in getting the book published. Laura knew Rissa had not been anywhere since the loss of her husband. She decided to be bold and asked Rissa if she would accompany her to a Christian Working Women's Conference in downtown Chicago in late May. Rissa told her friend she would think about it and let her know by the end of the week.

Things were a far cry from normal these days, but with the book for sale now, work stuff picking up, and planning the family beach trip to Saint Lucia, the overwhelming pain was very slowly subsiding. Later in the evening, she saw an email from Julie. Rissa opened it and could not believe what she was reading. Julie very politely asked Rissa if she would consider being a guest speaker at the Christian Working Women's Conference in Chicago later that month. Rissa closed her eyes and asked God what this was all about. She was a paralegal and a mom, not a conference speaker, especially in front of two thousand women. Rissa slept very little that night. She would lay awake, periodically pick up her phone, and open the Bible app. She read about Ruth, Hannah, and Esther, brave women who loved and obeyed God. She told God how these last several months had been exhausting and wondered how she was going to keep functioning. As she had done so many times before, she confided with the girls at dinner and told them of this latest challenge put before her. Staci, Jen, and Sadie one by one told their mom that this was the right thing to do. They knew their mom had the wisdom and courage to do this. She would talk from her heart and give the most touching speech that those women had ever heard.

Rissa prayed fervently and then decided to do it. She called Laura first and told her she was in but with a little twist. Rissa then called Julie and agreed to speak at the conference. They discussed a book appearance fee, and Julie set everything in motion. Rissa prepped for her speech in the evenings and on most weekends. The girls were terrific in listening to their mom practice as well as giving little hints here and there. Rissa, for the first time since the previous October, felt some peace; she was ready.

The conference opened up to a packed crowd, and the first few speakers were terrific. Rissa was nervous but also knew she could do this. With her lovely daughters and Laura sitting close to the stage, Rissa Boyer was introduced. Rissa looked out over the audience of all these women dressed in tailored business suits, stylish dresses, jeans, and blazers. Rissa started with telling the women she was a recent widow. She told of her husband's tragic accident and her daily struggle with grief and purpose. She described the painful conversations with her daughters at the dinner table those first few months. Rissa took her audience back in time and described how she had met this good-looking athlete at a local church years ago. She made the crowd laugh at the rather quick romance and then getting married six months later. She explained what it was like being married to a police officer and explained her fears of his dangerous profession. Her anxieties became a reality when David was shot in an alley on a cool October night. Rissa choked back tears describing the morning in the hospital when she first learned David was going to survive and she was not going to be a police officer's widow.

Rissa stopped for a second, then rather emphatically said, "Then God stepped in, revealing his plan for David."

"David was somehow gifted to experience heaven for a short time. David was blessed to remember his time with amazing detail and then put it into words—the final product being this book lying beside me here on this table." Rissa continued, "My publicist and now my good friend, Julie Peters, and I had a few tense conversations about how to market this book. Today is the first time I have ever spoken in public about *A Window into Heaven*. David did not write this story to sell books, to make a good profit—he wrote about this incredible true experience to simply tell others about Jesus. David saw Jesus through the lens of the angel Josiah. My daughters and I still grieve daily over the tragic loss of their father and my loving husband, who left us way before his time. Yet, God determined David's time. I often don't understand it, but I am learning to accept it. Staci, Jennifer, and Sadie don't understand it but somehow accept it. David loved being a police officer. He loved being a father to his girls and a wonderful husband to his wife. His love and passion for his honorable career and the people closest to him is what he would consider his legacy. I am learning every day that writing this book would also be part of his story, his legacy."

Rissa stopped again, wiped a few tears away. "As David was starting his story, we talked about the goals for his book. David said without hesitating, 'I saw God's inspiring creation, and I felt who God is. People need to know and believe it's all true: He is real! God is love and wants to be the center of our lives.'"

Rissa looked out over her audience, looked at her girls, then spoke. "You have seen this famous Bible verse at football games, John 3:16: 'For God so loved the world that he sent his one and only Son, that whoever believes in him shall not perish but have eternal life.' David saw this love, felt this love, and wrote this story so many would understand and believe it too."

Rissa exhaled and finished with, "Thank you and God bless you."

The crowd jumped to their feet in a thunderous standing ovation. The Boyer girls ran on stage and hugged their mom as tight as they had ever done so before.

Epilogue

In 2022 sales for *A Window into Heaven* exceeded $12 million, making it one of the top five best-selling Christian books in the 2000s. It won the Christy Award in 2022 for its excellence in Christian fiction.

Rissa, Staci, Jennifer, and Sadie Boyer are the founding trustees for the Sergeant David Boyer Foundation. The Boyer Foundation would open its faith-based horse ranch for teenage recovering addicts and at-risk youth outside Granby, Colorado, in 2023.

Nickolas Patros got promoted to chief petty officer and still serves on the USS *George H. W. Bush*.

Ashley Briggs accepted Christ at a Bible study at the University of Missouri and is pursuing her degree in communications.

Officer Mike Sullivan retired after twenty years of service in the Saint Louis Metropolitan Police Department. He is the co-founder and vice president of Blue Flag Security, a private security firm.

Jason and Julie Peters had their first child, a beautiful baby girl named Clarissa.

Acknowledgments

This story was written as a gift to family and friends. I hope as they read this, they understand God's gift to us. Romans 6:23 says, "The gift of God is eternal life in Christ Jesus our Lord."

Legacy could not have been written without the considerable assistance and encouragement from my family.

To my loving wife, Nyla, my best friend and tireless editor by my side.

To my beautiful daughters—Kacey, Brittney, and Lexy—thank you for your love and the special relationship we continue to have. Brittney, you get a special thanks for your North Carolina trip contribution.

To my following law enforcement friends, thank you for your time and expertise you provided:

- Retired lieutenant colonel Jerry Leyshock, SLMPD
- Retired major Daniel E. Howard, SLMPD
- Retired lieutenant Kimberly Haley, SLMPD

- Retired detective Alan Pergande, CPD

To my friends in the medical community, thank you for the tireless work you do and the knowledge you shared:
- Steven E. Ross, MD, MPH
- Denice Gibson, DNP, RN, CRNI, AOCNS

To my friend and pastor, Ross Richardson

To my Kansas Jayhawk friend, thank you for your service:
- USN—Retired ABH2 (AW) Zach Briggs

To my friends in the community and the wonderful insight you provided on horses:
- Tina Kaminski
- Dale Kaminski

To my paralegal advisor:
- Senior paralegal Debbie McGuire